The Big Re.  **W9-AMX-925**

The Big Reset

Gold Wars and the Financial Endgame

Willem Middelkoop

AUP

Cover design: Studio Ron van Roon, Amsterdam
Lay-out: Crius Group, Hulshout

Amsterdam University Press English-language titles are distributed in the US
and Canada by the University of Chicago Press.

ISBN	978 90 8964 599 9
e-ISBN	978 90 4852 219 4 (pdf)
e-ISBN	978 90 4852 220 0 (ePub)
NUR	781

To Moos and Misha

In the absence of the gold standard, there is no way to protect savings from confiscation through inflation. There is no safe store of value. If there were, the government would have to make its holding illegal, as was done in the case of gold. If everyone decided, for example, to convert all his bank deposits to silver or copper or any other good, and thereafter declined to accept checks as payment for goods, bank deposits would lose their purchasing power and government-created bank credit would be worthless as a claim on goods. The financial policy of the welfare state requires that there be no way for the owners of wealth to protect themselves. [...] This is the shabby secret of the welfare statists' tirades against gold. Deficit spending is simply a scheme for the confiscation of wealth. Gold stands in the way of this insidious process. It stands as a protector of property rights. If one grasps this, one has no difficulty in understanding the statists' antagonism toward the gold standard.

– Alan Greenspan, former Chairman of the Federal Reserve (1966)

Table of Contents

Prologue

One year before the fall of Lehman Brothers, my first book was published in the Netherlands (*Als de dollar valt – If the Dollar Collapses,* 2007). After studying the financial system for over ten years, I had come to the conclusion that a collapse of the unstable global financial system – and its mountain of debt – was 'only a matter of time'. After the house of cards collapsed just one year later, my life changed dramatically. Within a short period of time, I became a well-known personality in the Netherlands. I decided to quit my job as market commentator for the business channel *RTL Z* in order to focus on business opportunities arising from the new economic reality. I believed this new reality would entice investors to look seriously at investing in hard assets, especially gold and silver. We have seen precedents of this in every crisis for the last 300 years. I subsequently started a web shop for gold and silver bullion (AmsterdamGold.com) and set up a commodity fund (Commodity Discovery Fund). AmsterdamGold was sold to the listed Value8 in the summer of 2011, after yearly sales reached 100 million euros. In the same period, three more of my books became bestsellers. None of them were ever translated into English.

This book combines information from all previous books with an additional chapter on the expected Big Reset for the current worldwide monetary system. The book tells the story of a mostly hidden world of money and gold which I hope will also be of interest to a larger, international public.

Introduction

Before World War I, almost all major currencies were backed by gold. This was the era of the gold standard. The money supply was restricted to the growth of the gold supply. As European countries needed to create money in order to finance the high costs of the war, most were forced to abandon the gold standard in the 1910s. The gold standard was replaced by a fiat money system in most countries, although silver coins were still being used in most European countries until the 1980s.

Unlike fiat money, gold has always maintained its purchasing power. An old Roman aureus gold coin of just eight grams still buys you a few hundred liters of cheap wine, just as it did 2,000 years ago. That is why gold has been used again and again to stabilize fiat money systems during monetary resets in the past.

The gold price is like a barometer: a rise in the price acts as a warning to investors that something is wrong with their currency. Often it is a sign that bankers are creating too much money. Since the US took the dollar off the gold standard in 1971, gold has become financial enemy #1 of Wall Street and the White House. This is because the price of gold acts like a canary in the coalmine by pointing to a decline in the value of the dollar.

This book provides all the evidence needed in support of the claim that a secret war on gold (Chapter 4) has been fought by the US and other central bankers at least since the 1960s, when the dollar system came under pressure for the first time since its inception at the end of World War II.

Nowadays even the Swiss franc is no longer a safe currency. The Swiss Central Bank decreed in 2012 that its currency would be pegged to the euro to stem a further rise in value, which was considered harmful to Swiss tourism and exports. This is just one example of the currency wars that have been fought since the collapse of Lehman Brothers in 2008. More and more countries have been trying to debase their currencies to support their exports.

To combat the economic fallout caused by the credit crisis, countries have allowed their fiscal deficits to increase dramatically. In order to pay the bills, governments had to sell enormous amounts of bonds. As more and more investors stopped buying these government bonds, central banks needed to step up to the plate. By turning on the (digital) printing presses, they have been buying up bad debts and government bonds to a total of $ 10 trillion ($ 10,000 billion) worldwide, between 2008 and 2013. Economists describe this process as the monetization of debt by central banks. Economic textbooks refer to this process as 'the nuclear option' – only to be used when no other method of financing can be applied effectively. This is a process that is easy to start but almost impossible to stop.

Universities worldwide still promote the ideas of the Chicago School of Economics. The tenet of the Chicago School is based on the creation of fiat money by central banks in collaboration with private banks. Students today still use the same economics textbooks with outdated models based on efficient markets, just as they did before the crisis. That is why a majority of economists, journalists and business executives still do not fully understand the role of money in our economy.

I am not handicapped by a degree in economics, and I have always used my common sense to understand the principles of money. I have long learned to fall back on books about money and financial crises that are written by historians. The current crisis – which could have been predicted on the basis of roughly 6,000 years of the documented history of money – contradicts the Keynesian doctrine of creating money out of thin air. Fiat money systems have been put to the test more than 200 times, and they have all failed in the end. The likelihood of failure should now be considered a statistical certainty rather than a theoretical improbability.

At some point, politicians will start to understand that only a major change – a big reset, as I call it – in our global monetary system can save it. This realization will probably occur around the time that they are no longer able to refinance their mountains of debt.

This book explains why piling more and more debt onto the balance sheets of central banks is not a sustainable way of helping our economies recover. But policymakers will always choose a possible economic death in the future over a nigh certain economic death now. This demonstrates the inadequacy of our system, which focuses on treating the symptoms while ignoring the actual illness. The system is like a terminal patient who can only hope for a few more years of survival. Only by administering a cocktail of the strongest medicines can the patient stay alive. He will never be as strong as before, but by ever-increasing visits to the medicine cabinet he is able to delay the inevitable for a little while longer.

Central bankers and politicians are merely buying time, hoping to prolong the endgame phase of our global financial system as it exists today. But there are those who have secretly started to prepare for the big reset that is needed to bring this financial system to the next level. A similar reset took place with the start of the dollar system in 1944. It is my belief that, well before 2020, the global financial system will need to be rebooted to a new paradigm in which gold will play a larger role, the dollar will lose its status as the sole reserve currency, and countries like China will be much more powerful.

I would like to end by thanking Amsterdam University Press (AUP) and The University of Chicago Press for publishing this book, which is so critical of the 'Chicago School of Economics'. A special thank to Ebisse Rouw (AUP) who started it all. I also would like to praise my (research) assistants Dick van Antwerpen en Kevin Benning who helped me to dig up some wonderful details. Gioia Marini did a great job in editing the manuscript. The cover design shows Ron van Roon is a real artist. And a special thanks to my wife Brechtje Rood who was responsible for the infographics in this book and who supported me in every way during this stressful year. Finally, I thank you for taking the time to read it.

Willem Middelkoop, Amsterdam, January 2014

Chapter 1 – The History of Money

The few who understand the (money) system will either be so interested from its profits, or so dependent on its favors, that there will be no opposition from that class.
 – Rothschild Brothers of London, (1773-1855)

When you or I write a check there must be sufficient funds in out account to cover the check, but when the Federal Reserve writes a check there is no bank deposit on which that check is drawn. When the Federal Reserve writes a check, it is creating money.
 – From *Putting It Simply* by the Boston Federal Reserve Bank (1984)

There's no limit to central bank expanding its balance sheet in theory.
 – Dennis Lockhart, Chairman of the board of the Federal Reserve Bank of Atlanta (2012)

Inflation is a more fundamental danger than speculative investment. Some countries seem to be in the unusual situation where they are trying to create inflation. They will come to regret that.
 – Paul Volcker (2013)

The old saying is that 'figures will not lie,' but a new saying is 'liars will figure.' It is our duty, as practical statisticians, to prevent the liar from figuring; in other words, to prevent him from perverting the truth, in the interest of some theory he wishes to establish.
 – Carroll D. Wright, statistician addressing the Convention of Commissioners of Bureaus of Statistics of Labor (1889)

INTRO

Although we talk about money on a daily basis and most of us work hard for it, few stop to reflect on what money actually is and what it means. Even people working in the world of finance often do not comprehend what money is all about. The fact that money is created out of thin air and in the form of credit is quite difficult to understand. This important little secret is not taught at most schools and is actually only understood by a confined group of financial insiders. This is not necessarily a bad thing. According to Henry Ford, the famous car manufacturer, a revolution would break out before dawn if people got wind of how our money system really works.

1.   What is the origin of money?

Ten thousand years ago, money in the form that we know it, did not exist. A simple community consuming merely a few varieties of food and materials, did not need a trading system. However, as soon as society began to develop, the demand arose for a more complex trading system. What developed out of this demand was a system of barter and exchange and even credit. Desired products that were relatively stable in value, like cattle and dried meat, were used more and more frequently as a method of payment.

Bartering is still the most elementary system of trade. In times of crisis, this form of commerce is frequently re-introduced. Towards the end of World War II, cigarettes were a much-used means of barter on the devastated European continent. In effect, cigarettes were transformed from consumption goods into 'preferred goods with the function of money', in economist speak.[1] In Argentina in 2001, when foreign powers refused to lend money to the country anymore and the national financial system collapsed, bartering emerged within 24 hours. And as recently as 2013, Iran delivered oil to China and India in exchange for gold.[2] Iran was forced to barter due to an economic boycott by the US and the EU which had shut Iran out of the international SWIFT payment system from 2012 to 2013, preventing the country from carrying out international payments.

Bartering has many disadvantages. There is not always a constant need for certain products, and perishable goods are unstable in value.

Large, round Rai-stones were used as a means of exchange (money) approximately 600 years ago on the Micronesian island of Yap. The biggest Rai that was ever found was three metres in

---

1   Extensively described by R. A. Radford in 'The Economic Organization of a Prisoner of War Camp', Economica, Year 12, nr. 48, 1945, p. 189-201.
2   http://www.bbc.co.uk/news/business-17203132

diameter and weighed 4,000 kilograms. The stones were rare because they had to be brought from the islands of Palau, which lie 400 kilometres away. Transporting the stones brought great risks with it. Up to this very day, the stones are valid as a form of barter. Other much-used means of exchange were shells (China) and grain (Mesopotamia, Babylon and Egypt).

2.   How did gold become money?

Obviously, it is possible for some goods to act as money. These goods do need to have certain characteristics: they have to be easily divisible, portable, imperishable and scarce. But if you wish to exchange, calculate and save it – three functions that are essential in an efficient society – then money has a good deal of important advantages over valuable goods.

Since 700 B.C., the peoples of almost all cultures – Mayans, Incas, Egyptians, Greeks, Romans, Byzantines, Ottomans and Arabs – have considered gold and silver to be a valuable means of exchange. And because of their unique characteristics, scarcity and attraction, these precious metals have formed the basis of monetary systems around the world for thousands of years.

Apart from being divisible, portable, enduring and scarce, precious metals are enormously desirable. Whether that is due to their shine or weight (gold weighs almost twice as much as lead), people all over the world feel attracted to gold and silver. In addition, gold and silver are impossible to copy. Out of the entire periodic table of elements, gold and silver are the most suitable as a means of payment.

Precious metals also turn out to be perfect stores of value. Proof of the fact that gold has around the same value as 2,000 years ago can be found in the Museum of London. On display is a Roman *aureus* coin, which contains eight grams of 22-carat (90%) gold. According to the details printed next to it, one *aureus* could buy some 400 liters of cheap wine. At 2011 prices, eight grams of 22-carat gold is worth roughly 400 euros. When bought in small cartons at French wine houses, one can still buy wine for around one euro per liter. The demand for gold and silver is infinite and eternal.

3.   When did coins come into existence?

The first form of coined money can be dated back to China. Around the same time, coins appeared in the West and in India. The Chinese coins were minted from various metals, including copper and bronze. The coins were made under strict supervision by the government in order to guarantee uniformity. Since the Chinese made their coins from base metals, their money had a low intrinsic value.[3] It is for this reason that a hole was bored into the middle of the coin so that a large number of coins could be transported on a string. Chinese money had low production costs but had the disadvantage that it was easy to replicate.

The first Western coins originated in Lydia, in today's western Turkey, around 650 B.C. They were made from electrum, a natural alloy of gold and silver. Thanks to the invention of a standard by which the purity of gold and silver could be established, the coins were quickly split into gold and silver variants. Because gold is about fifteen times more rare, silver was used for coins with a low nominal value.[4]

Alexander the Great, Julius Caesar and Emperor Augustus all built their empires around a monetary system based on gold. Maintaining the value of one's currency was key to keeping power. Soldiers were kept happy by regular payments of wages in gold and silver coins. Whenever the value of the currency was undermined, the empire came under pressure. There are strong indications that the Roman Empire fell because the Roman currency was debased. Following the demise of significant sources of income, the most important Roman coin fell considerably in value between 238 A.D. and 274 A.D. due to the silver content

---

3   The intrinsic value of a coin is determined by the value of the metal with which the coin is made. http://www.investorwords.com/2587/intrinsic_value.html
4   The nominal value refers to the value that is shown on the coin.

being continually reduced.[5] It is no coincidence that an economic crisis then ensued.[6]

Silver content Denarius ────────────────────────

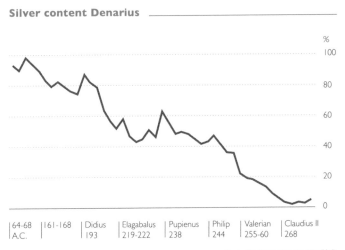

Source: Zerohedge/ Tulane university (2010)

5   http://www.tulane.edu/~august/handouts/601cprin.htm
6   'The Crisis of the Third Century (234–284 A.D.)', http://en.wikipedia.org/wiki/Decline_of_the_Roman_Empire. http://en.wikipedia.org/wiki/Crisis_of_the_Third_Century.

4. A short history of monetary gold

After the fall of the Roman Empire, Western Europe returned to a locally organized economy where barter once again became the norm.[7]

During the Middle Ages, the Byzantine gold solidus coin, commonly known as the bezant, was used widely throughout Europe and the Mediterranean. The bezant was possibly the most successful means of payment in world history. These gold coins existed from 491 A.D. to 1453 A.D. and were accepted as money from England to China.[8] In 1252, gold coins called florins were minted in Genoa and Florence for the first time in almost five hundred years. The florin was the precursor to the Dutch guilder, which was used all the way up until 1999.[9] Shortly afterwards, Venice introduced the ducat which had the same size and weight as the florin. Towards the end of the 13th century, all Italian city states, whose influence was rapidly increasing, made use of gold coins in order to facilitate their growing trade, thereby toppling the monarchs' monopoly on the issuance of money. In a short time frame, these gold coins spread throughout Western Europe, spawning a monetary system based on gold. In 1275, eight silver coins were needed to buy one gold coin of the same weight.

After the decline of the Byzantine Empire, and the spread of the bubonic plague and a series of financial crashes hammered Europe, the role of the bezant as money was replaced by silver coins in many European countries. From 1550 until the early 17th century, a long period of general price increases ensued. After the discovery of large deposits of silver in Latin America in the 16th century, an international silver standard developed, which

---

7   B. Bartlett, 'How Excessive Government Killed Ancient Rome', in: *The Cato Journal*, year 14, no 2, 1994.

8   Antony Sutton, *The War on Gold.*

9   R. Kool, 'A Thirteenth Century Hoard of Gold Florins From the Medieval Harbour of Acre', in: The Numismatic Chronicle 166, 2006.

existed for almost 400 years. Since silver has less value than gold, silver coins were more easy to use for every day purchases. A silver standard was also adopted by the United States in 1785.

In the period between 1750 and 1870, many wars were fought on the European continent. Because of this and also due to ongoing trade deficits with China, a significant amount of silver moved eastwards, causing many silver standards to disappear over time.

Economic history of China and other major powers _____

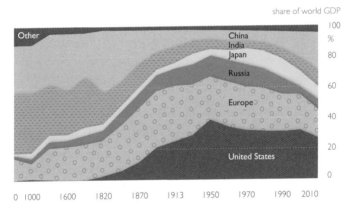

Source: University of Groningen

5. What are the advantages of a gold standard?

Within a gold standard, each unit of money (one hundred euro, for example) corresponds to a certain amount of gold (say, 2 grams). A currency's value is backed by gold bars in the vault of the government or the central bank.

Having a gold standard brings with it many advantages. The most important advantage is that it forces governments to be disciplined in their fiscal policy because they cannot turn on the printing press to finance budget deficits.

Gold offers monetary security and is the most important weapon against the depreciation of money. A gold standard gives citizens economic freedom because their money is always exchangeable for gold. Gold is recognized worldwide as being valuable and for this reason, citizens are not dependent on financial decisions made by financial authorities, as is the case today. An undisciplined buildup of credit and debt – the real origin of the current credit crisis – cannot occur within a gold standard.[10]

Due to the mounting silver shortages, the United Kingdom and many countries in the British Empire adopted a gold standard in 1816. They were soon followed by Canada (1853), the US (1873) and Germany, where the new gold mark was introduced in 1872. In the course of the 19th century, the gold standard became more and more popular.

The stability of prices over a long period of time can be attributed to the disciplinary monetary effect of a gold and/or silver standard. England, for example, experienced almost no inflation for almost two hundred years up until the dissolution of the gold standard in 1914.

10   Gold standard: http://economics.about.com/cs/money/a/gold_standard.htm.

When money printing is not an option, even fighting wars is made more difficult.[11] The period between 1850 and 1914 – when most European countries were on a gold standard – was a time of economic prosperity in Europe during which no major wars took place.

The value of the dollar remained stable as long as the US had a gold standard.

---

11   Wars are frequently financed with fiat money and, partly for that reason, they put the monetary systems of warring countries under pressure. This was certainly the case with the First World War, the war in Vietnam and the Iraq-Afghanistan War.

6.   Why was the gold standard abandoned?

With a gold standard, politicians and bankers have little influence over the economy because they are unable to influence the exchange rates of the currency. It is also not possible to print money to supply 'easy credit' to businesses in an effort to kick-start the economy, as is the standard monetary procedure nowadays.

A gold standard does not collapse or disintegrate on its own. When a large trade deficit occurs, gold reserves can be drained pretty quickly. When these large outflows occur, countries cannot guarantee that their currency will remain exchangeable for gold and are often forced to withdraw from a gold standard. This is precisely what happened to the US in 1971.

Many European countries went off the gold standard in 1914 in order to be able to print more money to finance the First World War. Wartime governments understand that they cannot raise money to finance the war by raising taxes or by borrowing from banks. Accelerating the printing presses is an easier method – and often the only way – to pay for a war.

After the end of World War I, the excessive money creation continued apace, leading to the creation of a massive credit bubble in the 1920s. This led eventually to the market crash of 1929, after which the world economy collapsed and fell into a deep economic crisis.

7.   What is fiat money?

In a financial system where money is not backed by something substantial like gold or silver, banks can create virtually limitless amounts of money by creating new loans. All money is created in the form of credit (new debt). If all loans were to be paid off, all money would disappear. Because interest has to be paid on every loan, however, more and more new money (i.e. debt) has to be created. We call money that is created during this process of unbacked money creation, *fiat* or *fiduciary* money. Its value rests on the confidence that goods or services can be paid for. The term fiat refers to the first words that God spoke according to the story of Genesis in the Bible: 'Fiat lux' in Latin, or 'Let there be light' in English.

All known fiat money systems have failed in the past (see Appendix I). Central bankers, however, continue to claim that this time, all will be well. Such claims are reminiscent of the joke about the guy who jumps from the roof of an 80-story building. As he flies past the 20th floor, somebody shouts from the window to inquire whether all is fine. 'No problems so far!' is the answer. If turning on the printing presses would lead to prosperity, then Africa would not be a poor continent, Zimbabwe would be rich and the Weimar Republic would still exist.

8.   What is meant by fractional banking?

In a fractional reserve banking system, the bank retains only a portion of all outstanding liabilities as available reserves. In 1900 this was around 30%, and has now declined to just 3%.

Fractional banking started at the end of the Middle Ages, when Italian bankers[12] – often goldsmiths – started to give 'bills of exchange' to clients who stored their gold coins with them. These bills were used more and more as money, since they were backed by gold. When bankers noticed that the gold coins were hardly ever retrieved from their bank safes, they began giving out more of these receipts than could be backed by the gold in their vaults. These receipts are considered to be the first bank notes.

Nowadays, bank reserves are held as currency or as a deposit with the central bank. Commercial banks can take out loans from the central bank based on assets on their books. The money for this new loan is created out of thin air and credited to the commercial bank's account at the central bank. Now the bank can use this new money to fund new loans or investments.

So money creation starts at the central bank. By typing a few numbers on the computer, unlimited amounts of new money can be created. If, for instance, 10 billion is created this way, then this amount will be transferred from the central bank to a commercial bank.[13] The receiving bank can then sell loans to the value of 90% of this 10 billion. The amount of 9 billion is transferred onto another bank's account and this party will lend out another 90% of the 9 billion (= 8,1 billion). This process can continue until the original 10 billion from the central bank has generated extra credit in the amount of more than 90 billion. This is the theory known as fractional banking.

---

12   The oldest bank in the world, the Monte dei Paschi di Siena (1472), has come into serious trouble a few years after the start of the current credit crisis.

13   In exchange for collateral, like a package of old loans.

A commercial bank can thus create new money by selling a new loan and putting it on its balance sheet. In practice, banks try to lend out as much money as possible and will search for the cheapest possible funding. It is important to understand that central banks can never replenish the reserves of a bank. They can increase a commercial bank's liquidity but never its solvency.

Solvency of Dutch banks 1900-2010

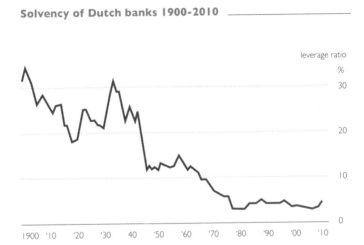

source: DNB

9. Where was fiat money invented?

As with many other inventions, fiat money was first invented in China.[14] Marco Polo, who travelled extensively throughout the Far East from 1275 to 1292, published a book describing his travels after returning to Italy. For Europeans, his texts were the only source of information about Asia for many centuries. Polo described how the leader at that time, the Emperor Khan, had found a way of creating paper money that was just as valuable as gold and silver.[15] His Mongol Empire reached from Siberia to the Black Sea, covering around one-fifth of the world's inhabited land area:[16]

> You might say the Emperor has the secret of alchemy in perfection, and you would be right. The Emperor makes his money of the bark of a certain tree, in fact of the mulberry tree, the leaves of which are the food of the silkworms, these trees being so numerous that the whole districts are full of them. What they take is a certain fine white bark or skin which lies between the wood of the tree and the thick outer bark, and this they make into something resembling sheets of paper, but black. When these sheets have been prepared they are cut up into pieces of different sizes. All these pieces of paper are issued with as much solemnity and authority as if they were of pure gold or silver; and on every piece a variety of officials, whose duty it is, have to write their names, and to put their seals. And when all is prepared duly, the chief officer deputed by the Khan smears the seal entrusted to him with vermilion, and impresses it on the paper, so that the form of the seal remains imprinted upon it in red; the money is then

14 G. Davies, *A History of Money*, p. 49-54.
15 Marco Polo, *Il Milione*. (2001)
16 http://www.allempires.com/article/index.php?q=The_Mongol_Empire

authentic. Anyone forging it would be punished with death. And the Khan causes every year to be made such a vast quantity of this money, which costs him nothing, that it must equal in amount all the treasure of the world. With these pieces of paper, made as I have described, he causes all payments on his own account to be made; and he makes them to pass current universally over all his kingdoms and provinces and territories, and whithersoever his power and sovereignty extends. And nobody, however important he may think himself, dares to refuse them on pain of death. And indeed everybody takes them readily, for whosesoever a person may go throughout the great Khan's dominions he shall find these pieces of paper current, and shall be able to transact all sales and purchases of goods by means of them just as well as if they were coins of pure gold. Furthermore all merchants arriving from India or other countries, and bringing with them gold or silver or gems and pearls, are prohibited from selling to anyone but the emperor. He has twelve experts chosen for this business, men of shrewdness and experience in such affairs; these appraise the articles, and the emperor then pays a liberal price for them in those pieces of paper. And with this paper money they can buy what they like anywhere over the empire. So he buys such a quantity of those precious things every year that his treasure is endless, while all the time the money he pays away costs him nothing at all.

The Mongol Il-Khans in Persia, impressed by the use of paper money in China since 1024, decided to adopt this system. Technical advisers were sent to Peking, and an organization to introduce fiat money was set up. The Persian people, however, had not been able to grow gradually accustomed to the use of paper currency over several hundred years of incremental developments. They simply refused to believe that these nicely printed pieces of paper were worth anything, and the experiment ended in failure.[17] Paper money in Asia disappeared from the 14th century onwards. A great thirst for silver followed. Almost 25% of the world population was living in China at that time. Paper money would not reappear until 1609, when the Wisselbank in Amsterdam started issuing 'bills of exchange'.

17   Gordon Tullock, Political Economist (1957).

10.   Other examples of fiat money throughout history

Over 400 years later, in 1716, the Scottish economist John Law managed to convince the French King to conduct an unparalleled monetary experiment. Law was the son of a banker and travelled throughout Europe as a financial expert hoping to win rulers over to his economic ideas. He understood that a country could stimulate the economy through means of fiat money.

France was on the edge of an abyss due to the many wars of the Sun King, Louis XIV. The French regent[18] allowed John Law to set up a bank with restricted powers to issue bank notes. Through its success, the bank quickly grew to become the Banque Générale, and the money that it issued was even elevated to legal tender.[19] Large volumes of money were pumped into the economy this way, which did indeed stimulate the French economy.

Law eventually got himself into trouble pursuing another business opportunity. In 1717, he founded the Mississippi Company. His company received monopoly rights on trade between France and the French colony Louisiana in the south of the US. Thanks to a promotional campaign about the unlimited possibilities of the new promised land, more and more French people bought shares in the new company. But the speculation turned into a hype and got out of control. The boom turned into a bust and both experiments failed: the share price of his new company and the value of the fiat money plunged. Law's life in France was no longer safe and so he fled to the Netherlands. In 1726, with the permission of the Dutch government, he succeeded in setting up the first national lottery.

18   http://www.historyworld.net/wrldhis/plaintexthistories.asp?
paragraphid=kbb
19   Similar to American bankers, who christened their central bank 'The Federal Reserve', Law knew that a confidence-inspiring name partly determines the success of a bank.

11. Other misfortunes with fiat money

Hardly a century later, it all went wrong again. In the years after the French Revolution, the Assemblée Nationale issued national bonds, so-called 'assignats'. The suggestion was planted that these bonds, which were also used later as money, were backed by the church's possessions that had been confiscated during the Revolution in 1779. According to a government report from 1790, an attempt was made to stimulate the economy by turning on the printing press:

> We have to save the country and the even greater amounts of money shall help France to recover.[20]

We might well call this Quantitative Easing[21] (QE) avant la lettre.

Because of all this newly printed money, people began to distrust paper money. The French government quickly implemented some strict new rules. Maximum prices were set to curb inflation, and it was forbidden on pain of death to ask to be paid in gold instead of paper money when selling goods. In a last attempt to protect the paper money system, all trade in precious metals was forbidden as of 13 November 1793. These measures, however, only delayed the inevitable. As history has shown time and again, rulers have yet to succeed in printing extra money with impunity or to implement the 'conjure-something-out-of-nothing' trick with lasting success.

In mid-August 1796, after a few years of financial disarray, the lack of public confidence in the French currency reached an apex, and hyperinflation ensued. Soon, paper money lost all value. The people's anger was so intense that mobs gathered in the Place Vendôme to publicly burn paper money, printing plates

---

20 Antony Sutton, *The War on Gold.*
21 Quantitative easing will be explained extensively in the following section.

and money presses.[22] Due to the subsequent hyperinflation, many years of chaos ensued. After this monetary disruption, Napoleon introduced a bimetallic monetary system which restored financial stability from 1803 onwards. Most of Europe joined this monetary system. The new French franc remained in existence for almost two hundred years, until the introduction of the euro.[23] In 1865, several European countries created the first European monetary union (known as the Latin Monetary Union). It was disbanded in 1927 and the bimetallic system was repealed in 1928.

22   Richard M. Ebeling, 'The Great French Inflation', in: *The Freeman*, year 57, nr. 6, 2007.
23   But because the French government was forced to keep printing money to be able to cover the costs of World War I, in 1914 it stopped pegging the franc to gold.

12. What is Quantative Easing?

Quantitative easing (QE) is the euphemistic term used by the US Federal Reserve to build a smokescreen around the unconventional monetary policies it has embarked upon. If QE were a patriotic military operation, it would probably have been named 'Operation Firing up the Printing Press'. But since this would endanger public trust in the value of the currency, the spin doctors at the Fed decided on the term Quantative Easing. Only one in a million would understand that QE has to do with printing more money.

Before he became Fed Chairman, Ben Bernanke mentioned the possibility of turning on the printing presses in order to fight deflation:[24]

> The US government had a technology called the printing press (or, today, its electronic equivalent), so that if rates reached zero and deflation threatened, the government could always act to ensure deflation was prevented.

Central banks only embark on these unorthodox monetary policies to stimulate the economy when standard monetary policies have become ineffective.

Wikipedia defines QE in the following way:

> A central bank implements quantitative easing by buying specified amounts of financial assets from commercial banks and other private institutions, thus increasing the monetary base. This is distinguished from the more usual policy of buying or selling government bonds in order to keep market interest rates at a specified target value.[25]

24 http://www.gpo.gov/fdsys/pkg/GPO-FCIC/pdf/GPO-FCIC.pdf
25 http://en.wikipedia.org/wiki/Quantitative_easing#cite_note-39

With quantitative easing, central banks provide commercial banks with excess liquidity to promote private lending. Japan's central bank, the Bank of Japan (BOJ), is seen as the inventor of these recent unconventional strategies. During the middle of the 1990s, Japan experienced a severe recession after years of economic partying in the 1980s. The BOJ wanted to lower interest rates to zero. This was accomplished by buying more and more government bonds. Subsequently, the BOJ also bought asset-backed securities and equities.

Since the start of the global financial crisis in 2007, similar policies have been used by the United States, the United Kingdom and the Eurozone. As in Japan, the initial purpose was to lower interest rates. But from 2008 onwards, the Fed and other central banks started aggressively expanding their balance sheets by buying up assets such as Treasuries (US government bonds) and mortgage-backed bonds in order to support the housing market and to finance the large fiscal deficits that arose as a result of the economic fallout from the credit crisis.

The United Kingdom also used quantitative easing to support the British economy. Stephen Hester, CEO of the RBS Group, explains:[26]

> What the Bank of England does in quantitative easing is it prints money to buy government debt, and so what has happened is the government has run a huge deficit over the past three years, but instead of having to find other people to lend it that money, the Bank of England has printed money to pay for the government deficit. If that QE hadn't happened then the government would have needed to find real people to buy its debt. So the Quantitative Easing has enabled governments, this government, to run a big budget deficit without killing the economy because the Bank of England has financed it. Now you can't do that for long

26 http://www.itv.com/news/2012-05-11/hester-quantitative-easing-funds-bigger-budget-deficit/

because people get wise to it and it causes inflation and so on, but that's what it has done: money has been printed to fund the deficit.

Officially, central banks in most developed nations are prohibited from buying government debt directly. So they use a backdoor trick to buy their national bonds in the secondary market. In this two-step process, the government first sells bonds to private banks and insurers. These entities then sell these assets to the central bank.

13.   Do all central bankers agree on QE?

At least one central banker seems to be hedging against the risks of 'the biggest bond bubble' in history. Records show that Dallas Federal Reserve President Richard W. Fisher owns at least $ 1 million in gold in a portfolio[27] worth at least $ 21 million. This is apparently a hedge against the Fed's controversial QE policies, which he is surprisingly candid about:[28]

> It will come as no surprise to those who know me that I did not argue in favor of additional monetary accommodation during our meetings last week. I have repeatedly made it clear, in internal FOMC deliberations and in public speeches, that I believe that with each program we undertake to venture further in that direction, we are sailing deeper into uncharted waters. The truth, however, is that nobody on the committee, nor on our staffs at the Board of Governors and the twelve Banks, really knows what is holding back the economy. Nobody really knows what will work to get the economy back on course. And nobody – in fact, no central bank anywhere on the planet – has the experience of successfully navigating a return home from the place in which we now find ourselves. No central bank – not, at least, the Federal Reserve – has ever been on this cruise before.

He warned as early as 2010 that the Fed was 'positioning itself as the buyer of pretty much all government debt'. At that time, he described the risk of these unorthodox monetary policies as 'the risk of being perceived as embarking on the slippery slope of debt monetization'.

27   http://economix.blogs.nytimes.com/2012/01/31/how-the-fed-presidents-assets-stack-up/?_r=0
28   http://www.moneynews.com/StreetTalk/fed-fisher-inflation-qe3/2012/09/23/id/457266

He is not the only central banker who has been so candid about the risks of the worldwide strategy of quantitative easing. In a testimony before the Treasury select committee in 2013, the Bank of England's Executive Director of Financial Stability, Andy Haldane, said that the bursting of the bond bubble 'created by central banks forcing down bond yields by pumping electronic money into the economy' was the main risk to financial stability:

> If I were to single out what for me would be the biggest risk to global financial stability right now, it would be a disorderly reversion in the yields of government bonds globally. Let's be clear. We've intentionally blown the biggest government bond bubble in history. We need to be vigilant to the consequences of that bubble deflating more quickly than we might otherwise have wanted.

But the risk of inflating the international monetary system by printing too much money should also be considered. In the past, these kinds of monetary policies have led to periods of hyperinflation.

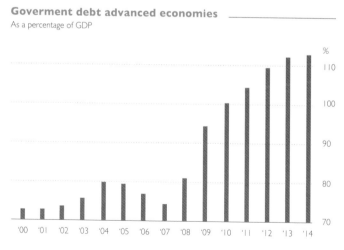

Goverment debt advanced economies
As a percentage of GDP

source: IMF and Fulcrum Asset Management

14.   When did hyperinflation occur?

One of the worst things that can happen to an economy is hyperinflation. The definition of hyperinflation is a rise in prices of over 50% within a year. Hyperinflation is so harmful because money loses its value and power. We could well call it the death of money. Without money, the economic system disintegrates and people revert almost immediately to bartering.

A good example of the dangers of fiat money is the hyperinflation that scourged Germany's Weimar Republic in the beginning of the 1920s. The German Republic stood under enormous financial pressure due to the huge amount of reparations imposed on it by the victorious Allies after the First World War. There was simply no way the German economy could bring in enough money to fulfill these payments year after year. The only way to do so was to allow vast amounts of fiat money to be printed. When high inflation resulted in the German people losing trust in the stability and value of their money, Germany found itself in a disastrous spiral of hyperinflation. Where one originally paid 42 marks for one US dollar, in 1923 the exchange rate had skyrocketed to more than 5 billion marks per dollar. In barely three years, the German currency had become worthless and the monetary system had crashed.[29] A financial nightmare became reality.[30] Many Germans lost all their savings and hope, with some committing suicide as a result.

29   Thomas Noble, *Western Civilization Beyond Boundaries*, p. 826-829.
30   Ferguson, *When Money Dies* (2010).

Periods of hyperinflation, ending with monthly inflation rates of well over 5,000%

Country	Year
Hungary	1946
Zimbabwe	2008
Yugoslavia	1994
Germany (Weimar)	1923
China	1949

15. Can we trust official inflation figures?

Governments are very creative in adjusting economic data. In the US, the manipulation of key figures and economic indicators has been elevated to a work of art. Many analysts and commentators now question the official statistics. Bill Gross, who founded PIMCO, the largest bond asset management company in the world, called the officially published inflation figures (CPI) 'a con job'[31] and the way they were presented a 'deception'.

The calculation of inflation can be influenced by the method and the model used. A model can be customized in many ways. When economists talk about financial engineering, it is clear that more than one outcome can be generated from a certain model.

Inflation is calculated as the average change in the price of a composite basket of goods and services over a given period. This is supposed to indicate whether the cost of living is higher (inflation) or lower (deflation) than earlier measured. This method is not very reliable because the choice of what goes into the basket of goods is necessarily arbitrary. Not everyone will buy the same products included in the basket of goods, of course. Many products and services are not included at all in the Consumer Price Index (CPI). Local taxes, for example, are not included in the CPI but they have risen sharply in recent years. As a result, disposable income has been growing less than inflation and many people feel 'squeezed'.

Cheuvreux, an equity broker owned by one of the largest French banks, Crédit Agricole, published a report[32] as early as 2006 claiming that real inflation rates in the US were around 6.7% – a number close to the growth of the money supply – instead of the officially published figures of around 2%.

31 http://www.investorsinsight.com/blogs/john_mauldins_outside_the_box/archive/2008/06/09/fooling-with-inflation.aspx
32 http://www.gata.org/files/CheuvreuxGoldReport.pdf

In the last decade, the monetary authorities in the US have fought a 'hidden war' against inflation, to ensure that the financial markets would not be alarmed by growing inflation. The main measures used were:

- To maintain low gold prices;
- Change of the method used for the calculation of inflation;
- Stop publishing the US M3 money growth figure.

The same report explains why a rise in the official inflation rate is disadvantageous for the government:

- It increases the costs for the government, as pensions and other social benefits have to be adjusted annually for inflation.
- Rising inflation leads to higher interest rates and therefore higher borrowing costs for the government and higher mortgage rates for consumers. Higher interest rates have a negative impact on stocks and bonds.

16.   How is inflation calculated?

Statisticians have found a number of methods they can use to lower the official inflation figures. This covert war is conducted mainly by changing the calculation methodology of inflation. The statistical model was changed little by little over the past thirty years.

According to John Williams,[33] an economist who has specialized in this field, the quality of government statistics has deteriorated significantly since the 1990s. According to him, the statistics on inflation were fairly accurate until the early 1990s. In the following years, the model used to calculate inflation numbers started to change as politicians began to pressure the statisticians.

In his report 'The Consumer Price Index' from 2004, he lists the four most notable 'tricks' used:

1 – Replacement by cheaper alternatives
When a piece of meat is too expensive, it is replaced in the inflation model by a cheaper burger. This is justified by the argument that people will start looking for cheaper alternatives when prices rise.

2 – Geometric considerations
Over the years, the arithmetic weighting of items in the inflation basket was replaced by a geometric weighting. As a result, products rising in price weigh less heavily in the model while products that are cheaper are weighted more heavily.

3 – Hedonic adjustments
This is the strangest adjustment of all. It is used to lower prices in order to correct for quality improvements that are embedded in product prices (derived from the Greek word *hedone*, which means 'pleasure').

33   Founder of www.shadowstats.com
http://rationalwiki.org/wiki/Shadow_Government_Statistics

Not all of these methods have been misused, but the combination has had the result that inflation figures are structurally understated. With many entitlements tied to the Consumer Price Index (CPI), the real value of social security payouts has shrunk dramatically.

Is today's inflation manipulated? _____

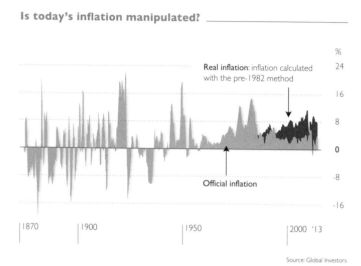

Source: Global Investors

Monthly inflation data going back for more than a century. The grey shaded areas represent the official Bureau of Labor Statistics' historical Consumer Price Index (CPI).

If we were to use the pre-1982 method of calculating CPI, we would end up with inflation as shown by the black line in the picture above. The black area shows that real inflation is currently around 8%. This compares to official statistics declaring CPI to be around 2%.

17. Examples of the distortion of inflation figures

The best example of a hedonic adjustment to price movements was highlighted in a Wall Street Journal article a few years ago. A TV model for sale for $ 30 in 2005 was being sold for the same price in 2006. But the model had slightly changed. The six-watt speaker had been changed to a ten-watt speaker, and the screen now had more rounded corners. Statisticians claimed that the television had become so much better that the price therefore should be adjusted downwards by 30% even if it was still being sold for the same price. These kinds of adjustments are being made continuously. The main consequence of all this is that people are not sufficiently compensated for the increased costs in their wages, pensions or benefits. Especially lower and middle class families are hurt by these changes.

From the government's perspective, another advantage to underestimating inflation is the way in which economic growth is adjusted for inflation. If an economy grows by 3% and inflation is 2%, then economic growth adjusted for inflation (known as real growth or real GDP) is 1%. But if inflation is in fact 4%, then in real terms the economy will have contracted by 1%. Adjusting for inflation can mean the difference between a recession and positive economic growth. Announcing that the economy is in a recession tends to lead to a decline in consumer confidence and also possibly lower consumer sales.

18.   Do central banks combat or cause inflation?

Central banks' websites often mention that all is about 'financial stability'[34] and that combating inflation is their main task. But they never tell you that they are the ones causing inflation by creating more and more money every year. Any student of monetary history knows that central bankers have never succeeded in building a lasting fiat money system without leading to a large loss in spending power. By printing more and more money, all currencies in a fiat money system are debased. According to former US Senator Ron Paul, the Fed's claim that it is fighting inflation is as incredible as cigarette manufacturers' statement that they want to help consumers stop smoking.[35]

Apart from fighting inflation, another vital task for most central banks is to stimulate the economy. This is why the amount of money in circulation has to grow each year. The goal of the ECB from its inception in the late 1990s was money growth of 4% to 5% annually. But within a few years after the introduction of the euro, yearly money growth had risen to above 10%. Through the excessive growth of debt, most Western currencies have lost over 95% of their spending power in the last century alone.

Central banks now also act as the lender of last resort. As a consequence, central banks such as the Fed and the ECB create over one trillion dollars in new money every year in order to support their governments. And still they claim they are fighting inflation.

34   During the Amsterdam Gay Pride of 2012, employees of the Dutch central bank danced around a see-saw upon which stood the word 'stability' in large letters.
35   Ron Paul, *End the Fed* (2009).

19. Does anybody really understand this financial system?

In most countries, governments and banks have worked together to monopolize the creation of money. The fact that our money is backed by nothing but hope and trust must be kept hidden from ordinary people. Even most economists do not fully understand money. Only those who have studied monetary economics know the inner workings of our financial system. And most of them end up working for their government or central bank, so they are bound to keep their mouths shut.

It suits bankers when consumers see a bank as a large piggy bank with lots of money in the safe. Few people know that printed and minted money represents only a small percentage of all the money that is in circulation. Research shows that, to this day, one-third of all people believe that vast piles of money lie waiting in the vaults of their bank for savers to go and collect. If savers realized the risks of their money being lent out over thirty times, they would probably prefer to buy gold. For this reason, it is of the utmost importance for banks to play down the safe-haven aspects of gold whilst simultaneously trying to maintain people's trust in money.

Savings in a bank account, however, are legally speaking a debt claim. That is why, in the case of a bank bankruptcy, deposits are not immediately returned to the deposit holder, as is the case with an equity or bond portfolio. In order to make sure that people do not withdraw their money en masse, the government guarantees the savings of every citizen up to the amount of 100,000 euros per bank in Europe and $ 250,000 in the US. Whether the government itself owns enough money to be able to cover these claims is, of course, questionable.

Most European bankers have allowed themselves to be completely hoodwinked by American propaganda that gold no longer plays an important role in the current financial system. In the Netherlands, almost all gold counters within banks have been closed. But in Switzerland you can still buy gold and silver at almost every bank.

Chapter 2 – Central Bankers: The Alchemists of our Time

The Bank hath benefited of interest on all monies which it creates out of nothing.
- William Paterson, one of the founders of the Bank of England (1697)

Gold still represents the ultimate form of payment in the world. Fiat money in extremis is accepted by nobody. Gold is always accepted.
- Alan Greenspan, former Chairman of the Federal Reserve (1999)

If the American people ever allow private banks to control the issue of their currency, first by inflation, then by deflation, the banks and the corporations which grow up around them will deprive the people of all property until their children wake up homeless on the continent their fathers conquered.
- Thomas Jefferson, third President of America and drafter of the Declaration of Independence (1808)

It is a sobering fact that the prominence of central banks in this century has coincided with a general tendency towards more inflation, not less. [I]f the overriding objective is price stability, we did better with the nineteenth-century gold standard and passive central banks, with currency boards, or even with 'free banking.' The truly unique power of a central bank, after all, is the power to create money, and ultimately the power to create is the power to destroy.
- Paul Volcker, former Chairman of the Federal Reserve in the foreword of *The Central Banks* (1995)

INTRO

The very first form of banking started well over 5,000 years ago, while fractional and fiat money systems began appearing almost 1,000 years ago. The first central bank appeared some 500 years ago. (Central) bankers, the alchemists of our time, have a monopoly on the creation of money, just like the police and army have a monopoly on violence. In the last century, central bankers have succeeded in turning paper into gold[36] and gold into paper.[37] The bank notes of the European Central Bank (ECB) no longer refer in any way to any intrinsic value, although the ECB still owns some 660 tonnes of gold. We have all become used to seeing unbacked paper money as value, which is precisely what our central bankers have been conditioning us to believe for over a century. Our entire monetary system is built on trust. Since the outbreak of this credit crisis, this trust has been waning rapidly worldwide. Even central banks have started buying gold to hedge the risks of their fiat own money system. Apparently, they also lack confidence in the long-term value of the dollar, still the world's reserve currency, and other fiat currencies.

36   On the first bank notes used in the Netherlands, a promise was printed that the bank would pay gold 'to the bearer of ten golden guilders'. Later on, that changed into 'to the bearer of 10 (silver) guilders', followed by 'to the bearer' and finally 'lawful means of payment'.

37   Since the 1980s, the price of gold has been determined by selling 'paper gold' on the futures markets. According to an LBMA study, total (paper gold) trading volume was a few hundred times the annual production of actual gold. (LBMA gold turnover survey Q1 2011, The Alchemist).

20.   When did the first form of banking emerge?

The history of banking could well be much older than is often thought. From archaeological finds, we know that a form of banking existed over 5,000 years ago. Clay tablets from around that time show transcripts of debt positions by farmers in southern Mesopotamia. Based on these findings, anthropologist David Graeber wrote a book entitled *Debt: The first 5,000 years* (2011) in which he claims that the first recorded debt systems were in the Sumer civilization around 3,500 B.C. in the region of what is now Iraq. In this early form of banking, farmers often became so mired in debt that they were periodically pardoned by kings who cancelled all debts. The Greeks and Romans also had financiers. In ancient China and India over 2,000 years ago, there were money lenders who sponsored farming projects, for example.

The first European banks appeared only in the early Middle Ages when goldsmiths also started to store the gold coins they were assessing for traders. At that time, merchants brought with them all sorts of gold and silver coins from abroad whose gold and silver content was not clearly known. The receipts for the stored coins soon became a form of money.

When the goldsmiths realized that the merchants often left their gold coins with them for long periods of time, the goldsmiths began to lend out the gold for a small fee, or 'interest'. Because the gold did not actually belong to the goldsmith and the risk therefore lay with the merchants, the latter received a portion of the interest. The rest was profit for the goldsmith. This activity was the first form of banking in Europe. The word 'bank' comes from the Italian word 'banca', the name used for the marble tabletop upon which Italian goldsmiths dropped foreign coins. From the sound of the coins being dropped, they could assess whether a coin contained a lot of copper or nickel.[38]

---

38   http://www.jamesrobertson.com/book/historyofmoney.pdf

Banks as we know them today were first set up during the Renaissance in the Italian cities of Florence, Venice and Genoa. The most famous is without doubt the Medici Bank, founded by Giovanni de' Medici in 1397. The oldest bank still in existence at the moment of writing is the Monte dei Paschi di Siena (1472), although it is currently fighting for its very survival.

When people realised that the profits that could be made from money lending as practiced by goldsmiths, more and more bankers sprung up. Only much later, after the decoupling of the gold standard, did bankers find out that lending fiat money – money created out of nothing – was even more profitable. Bankers do receive interest every month on all debts, after all.

21. How did central banking start?

During the Middle Ages, European royalty and even the church often needed to borrow money to fight wars. This financing was provided by so-called moneychangers. These early bankers also serviced travelling merchants when they needed to exchange foreign coins into local ones. As the size of the operations of moneychangers grew, they began to provide lending activities.

These moneychangers understood pretty quickly that lending to powerful entities such as kings and churches carried less risk because of the continual stream of income.

The German Rothschild family established an international banking business and dynasty, becoming one of the most powerful families in the 19th century. In return for financing royal empires, several family members were even elevated to nobility in Austria and the United Kingdom. At its height, the Rothschild family is believed to have possessed the world's largest private fortune by far.[39]

This can be seen as the start of modern banking. Often an intimate relationship developed between governments and bankers – one that can still be discerned today – and led to the establishment of the first central banks. Increasingly, bankers were given the right to print money in exchange for their financial support of the royal houses.

To this day, many central bankers regard politicians as loyal operators of the financial architecture they have been building for over 400 years. Over the years, bankers have learned that citizens could always be taxed by governments to pay back the banks. Moreover, banks know they will be bailed out if they run into trouble because the economy cannot function without them.

---

39 The family's wealth is believed to have declined subsequently because it had to be divided amongst hundreds of descendants. Now, Rothschild banking and investment businesses are much smaller than they were throughout the 19th century.

22.   The first central bank

In the early 17th century, the Dutch Republic was a powerful economic force in Europe, with Amsterdam as the capital of trade. At the time, over 800 different gold and silver coins were used in European trade, many damaged and worn. In order to value all the various coins and at the same time reduce the city's dependency on a number of moneychangers, the Amsterdam Wisselbank[40] was founded in 1609. It is frequently regarded as the first central bank.[41]

Within the Dutch Republic, 54 different mint masters had the right to mint gold and silver coins. The Wisselbank ensured that all coins that satisfied the quality requirements were accepted. The Amsterdam Wisselbank thus had a supervisory role but did not take action when issuing banks or institutions encountered problems. Its main function was the withdrawal of clipped,[42] doctored and counterfeit coins from circulation. They were melted and turned into coins that conformed to the quality requirements. Bills could be settled with bills of exchange, so coins could stay in the vaults of the Wisselbank. When customers exchanged their metal into paper currencies, they received a 5% premium. 35 years later, in 1644, Sweden would start the second central bank along this model, the Swedish Riksbank.

Most central banks in the past 400 years were initiated by rich businessmen who understood quite well that (central) banks, which owned the monopoly on creating money and were backed by government tax revenue, had a wonderful business model. But most central banks came under the control of the government

40   'Wissel' means exchange, so Wisselbank means exchange bank.

41   Stephen Quinn and William Roberds, 'An Economic Explanation of the Early Bank of Amsterdam, Debasement, Bills of Exchange, and the Emergence of the First Central Bank', *Working Paper Series* 2006-13, Federal Reserve Bank of Atlanta.

42   **Clipping** (shaving metal from the coin's circumference) and **sweating** (shaking the coins in a bag and collecting the dust worn off) were practices often used to exploit the value of gold and silver coins.

in the course of the 20th century. There are two exceptions to this. Half of the shares of the central bank of Belgium are still in the hands of private entities. And in the US, the American government does not own a single share in the Federal Reserve (Fed), which is owned entirely by affiliated banks. This explains why the Federal Reserve almost always champions what is good for banks on Wall Street.

23. Who created the first government bonds?

In the 1690s, the Scotsman William Paterson, who travelled throughout Europe just like John Law to spread his financial expertise, attempted to found an independent Scottish Empire in what is now Panama. He tried to sell the scheme to the governments of England, the Holy Roman Empire and the Dutch Republic, but none were willing to support him. After this failure, Paterson returned to London and made his fortune by setting up a business in trade with the West Indies.

In 1694, he wrote a pamphlet entitled *A Brief Account of the Intended Bank of England*. It explained how the British government could be helped to create money by setting up 'a joint-stock company' by the name of the 'Bank of England' to act as the English government's banker. He proposed a perpetual loan of £1.2 million to the government, but with an annual interest of 8% a year to the shareholders.[43] In return, the investors would be allowed to incorporate a 'Company of the Bank of England' with banking privileges, including the issuing of bank notes.

Paterson was backed by a group of rich traders from the City of London who would generate the starting capital. He was also supported by Charles Montagu, one of the most important officials within the Ministry of Finance. Together, they persuaded the government to create a bill so that the Bank of England could be established. The Royal Charter was granted on 27 July 1694. The first loan by the Bank of England was to finance the Royal Navy by issuing Navy Bills. British debt rose from one million pounds in 1688 to 48 million pounds in 1714. Over a quarter of taxes were used to fund the creation of the British Navy.

The start of the Bank of England is often seen as the start of a new era. Fiscal deficits by governments could be financed by means of selling (perpetual) bonds. We could in fact say that the

43   See the complete list of shareholders on: http://www.bankofengland.co.uk/about/Documents/pdfs/bankstock_transcript.pdf

current financial system of bond financings started with the foundation of the English central bank more than three hundred years ago.

24. How large has the bond bubble become?

The perpetual character of the first national loan was replaced in most countries by bonds with a duration of up to thirty years. Actually, these loans are almost never paid off but 'rolled over' continuously. New loans pay off old loans. Whoever sees this as a Ponzi scheme[44] is quite right.

This British model was so successful that other countries soon started their own private central banks. It all led to a mountain of government debt, which now totals around $ 50 trillion (as of 2012). There is no way this debt can ever be repaid in non-deflated currencies. Strangely enough, most of the money that is supposedly safely invested in risk-free bonds are most at risk.

Japan's external debt – i.e., the country's debt that has been borrowed from foreign lenders – has risen to almost 250% of GDP, while the external debt of the US is now on a parabolic move upwards. In Europe, the growth in the external debts of countries such as the United Kingdom, Greece, Portugal, Italy and Spain (and soon many others) is simply unsustainable. A recent study of eight centuries of government debt defaults by economists Carmen M. Reinhart and Kenneth S. Rogoff warns of the real likelihood of national debt crises in the near future.[45] We will look into this subject in more detail in chapter 4.

A global debt restructuring will probably be needed, and could be part of the Big Reset. In 2012, Bill Gross, founder of the largest bond investor house Pimco, advised investors to start buying 'hard assets' instead of paper assets such as government bonds.[46]

---

44 Named after the con man Charles Ponzi (1882-1949) who invented a system whereby payments are financed out of investments from new clients.

45 Carmen Reinhart and Kenneth Rogoff, *This Time is Different: Eight Centures of Financial Folly* (2009). http://scholar.harvard.edu/files/this_time_is_different_short.pdf

46 http://www.investopedia.com/stock-analysis/2012/bill-gross-says-to-buy-hard-assets-gsg-gld-gltr-rw00614.aspx

This is the equivalent of a car salesman advising people to start using the train instead of buying a new car.

Government Debts per country (2012, in US$)

United States	17,000 billion
EU total	16,000 billion
United Kingdom	10,000 billion
Japan	2,700 billion
Australia	1,500 billion
Switzerland	1,300 billion

US goverment debt / GDP ratio (1790-2013)

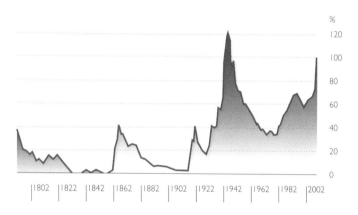

Source: Global Financial Data

25.   Who supervises central banks?

In a good functioning banking system, central banks keep a watchful eye over commercial banks to prevent them from taking irresponsible risks that could be harmful for the whole monetary system.

As we have learned, in the course of the 20th century, many governments took over central banks from private shareholders. Often, this was because politicians wanted to gain more control over the financial sector. Since then, central bankers have fought to gain more independence from politicians. Their main argument was and still is that it is far too dangerous when monetary policy is dependent on the short-term perspective of politicians. This often led to a compromise whereby central bankers work for the government but are granted a significant degree of autonomy in conducting monetary policy.

Initially, this independence worked rather well. But many Western central bankers have abused their freedom, often in collusion with private bankers, in order to increase their wealth and power. This is especially the case in the US.

Central bankers and private bankers have completely different mindsets. While the first are often academics and enjoy their position of power, private bankers are the real deal and moneymakers. As we have seen in the past, some will even sell their country for money. Napoleon stated in 1802:

> The hand that gives is above the hand that takes. Money
> has no motherland, financiers are without patriotism and
> without decency; their sole object is gain.

In the current banking system, central bankers often turn out to be lap dogs for private bankers instead of watch dogs. This explains how Wall Street banks were able to sell increasingly risky products (derivatives) without the US central bank standing in their way. Other central banks were pressured by the Fed to refrain from regulating the worldwide trade of derivatives. Not much has changed in the US since the start of the credit crisis. Annually, the financial sector spends about one million dollars per member of Congress on financial lobbying.[47]

47   http://www.opensecrets.org/lobby/
http://www.publicintegrity.org/2010/05/21/2670/five-lobbyists-each-member-congress-financial-reforms

26. Where are the most important decisions about the banking industry made?

Despite this collusion between central banks and commercial banks, politicians still believe that the best way to reform financial institutions is via self-regulation. The most important international banking regulations – known as 'the Basel Rules' – are still decided at regular meetings of the Bank for International Settlements (BIS) in Basel. The BIS can be seen as the mother of central banks and was founded at the International Bankers Conferences at Baden Baden (1929) and The Hague (1930).[48,49] The BIS was originally intended to facilitate the payment of reparations imposed on Germany by the Treaty of Versailles after World War I. But after hyperinflation in the Weimar Republic from 1921 to 1924, a new plan for settling German reparations was written in 1929.[50]

Between 1933 and 1945, the BIS board included Walther Funk and Emil Puhl, both high-level Nazis who were subsequently convicted of war crimes at the Nuremberg trials. After World War II, it became clear that the BIS, which had been a kind of house banker to the Nazis, had helped to launder stolen gold.[51] Under the supervision of Funk and Puhl, Nazi Germany had confiscated gold from Jewish concentration camp victims and melted it down to make new gold ingots. During the Bretton

---

48   James C. Baker, *The Bank for International Settlements*.

49   The famous historian Carroll Quigley writes about this in *Tragedy And Hope* (1966, p.278): 'The powers of financial capitalism had a far reaching aim, nothing less than to create a world system of financial control in private hands able to dominate the political system of each country and the economy of the world as a whole.'

50   The Young Plan reduced further payments to 112 billion Gold Marks, equivalent to US $ 8 billion in 1929 (US $ 109 billion in 2013) over a period of 59 years, which would end in 1988.

51   One of the main figures behind the establishment of the Bank for International Settlements in Basel in the 1930s was Halma Schacht, the central banker of Nazi Germany.

Woods conference of 1944, the bank was even accused of acting under orders from the Nazis. The Americans were appalled, and the US government supported a motion that called for the abolishment of the BIS. The proposal was supported by other European delegates but was opposed by John Maynard Keynes, the head of the British delegation. In April 1945, a decision to liquidate the BIS was made, but it was reversed by the US in 1948. The BIS had survived but was badly wounded. It had less influence and needed time to find a proper new role behind the scenes.

The BIS still operates as a counterparty, asset manager and lender for central banks and international financial institutions.

Switzerland agreed to act as the headquarter state for the BIS. The headquarters would be situated in Basel.

During the 1970s, the functions and the number of BIS members were substantially enlarged. Today, 60 central banks are members of the BIS, including those from the most important industrialized countries. Surprisingly, the Fed did not join until 1994.[52] This was because the Americans saw the BIS as a competitor to 'their' International Monetary Fund (IMF). At the start of the 1990s, the US realized they needed the BIS for European central bank support in its war on gold (of which more later) and in order to prevent regulation on derivatives.

While the presidents of the ECB and the Fed can still be held accountable by parliament or congress, no single form of democratic control exists over the decision-making process of the BIS. Their meetings are concealed from the outside world. Even ministers of finance have to guess what decisions bankers in Basel will take. The same bankers that brought our global financial system to the brink of collapse are deciding – behind the scenes and not answerable to anyone – on the banking reforms needed to prevent another credit crisis. It seems that not much has changed since the fall of Lehman.

52 http://www.bis.org/about/history.htm

To this day, BIS directors enjoy diplomatic status and cannot be prosecuted even after the end of their tenure. They are also allowed to move house with their family at any time to neutral Switzerland.[53]

53   www.bis.org/about/headquart-en.pdf

Chapter 3 – The History of the Dollar

Our American bankers have found that for which the ancient alchemists sought in vain; they have found that which turns everything into gold - in their own pockets; And it is difficult to persuade them that a system which is so very beneficial to themselves, can be very injurious to the rest of the community.

– William Gouge, A Short History of Paper-money and Banking in the United States (1833)

History shows that once an enormous debt has been incurred by a nation, there are only two ways to solve it: one is simply declare bankruptcy, the other is to inflate the currency and thus destroy the wealth of ordinary citizens.

– Adam Smith

Rising prices of precious metals and other commodities are an indication of a very early stage of an endeavor to move away from paper currencies. We have at this particular stage a fiat money which is essentially money printed by a government and it's usually a central bank which is authorized to do so. Some mechanism has got to be in place that restricts the amount of money which is produced, either a gold standard or a currency board, because unless you do that, all of history suggest that inflation will take hold with very deleterious effects on economic activity... There are numbers of us, myself included, who strongly believe that we did very well in the 1870 to 1914 period with an international gold standard.

– Alan Greenspan, former chairman of the Federal Reserve Board, (2011)

27.   How did central banking get started in the US?

Many of the Founding Fathers were strongly opposed to the formation of a central bank because England had tried to place the American colonies under the control of the Bank of England.

Robert Morris, a former government official, founded the first central bank in the US in 1781. He is seen as the father of the system of credit in the United States. His Bank of North America was based on the model of the Bank of England and could create as much money as needed through fractional reserve banking. Interestingly, the bank's collateral was a large quantity of gold that France had lent to the US. Morris' choice for his bank's name was a smart one: it led people to think they were dealing with a governmental bank, while in actual fact it was a private enterprise that had a monopoly on money creation.

Ten years later, after a compromise with Southern lawmakers, the name was changed to the First Bank of the United States (1791–1811). Several Founding Fathers were opposed to the Bank. Thomas Jefferson saw it as a venture for speculation, manipulation and corruption.[54] In 1811, its charter expired and was not renewed by Congress. In 1816, the government authorized the establishment of the Second Bank of the United States. The charter was not renewed in 1836 after a period of runaway inflation which led to a four-year-long depression in 1837. Between 1837 and 1862, only state-chartered banks existed. During this free banking era, many banks were short-lived with an average lifespan of five years.

The American people were against a central bank in private hands because they believed that the crises of 1873, 1893 and 1907 had been caused by the operating methods of international bankers. They also feared that too much power would be concentrated on the East Coast of America. Unfortunately, we now know that they were right.

54 http://en.wikipedia.org/wiki/History_of_central_banking_in_the_United_States

28.   When was the Federal Reserve created?

John Pierpont Morgan was the most famous and powerful banker of the early 1900s. After he was compelled to use his private fortune to stem the banking panic of 1907, he decided it was time for a new financial architecture. Soon, New York bankers came up with a brilliant idea. Their idea was start a new central bank that would be run and owned by New York bankers.

By this time, the US was the only major country without a central bank. In November 1910, Republican senator Nelson W. Aldrich joined a number of the most powerful Wall Street bankers for a secretly organized, private ten-day conference on Jekyll Island, the private island of J.P. Morgan. There was only one topic on the agenda: the establishment of a new central bank.[55]

It was agreed that this bank had to gain the monopoly on printing dollars and should become a private organization owned by the founders (Wall Street bankers). To the outside world, it would not be called a central bank and would act as if it was operated by the government.[56]

In order to allow the Aldrich[57] plan to succeed, it had to first be heavily promoted among the people and the government. As illustrated above, the establishment of two earlier central banks had ended in fiascos. This may explain why, despite Wall Street's best efforts, the members of the US House of Representatives did not support the Aldrich plan.

Then, during the elections of 1912, a wind of change blew through Washington. Although the Republicans once again presented their plan for establishing a central bank, it was the Democrats who presented the Federal Reserve Act, also in co-

55   Eustace Mullins, *The Secrets of the Federal Reserve*, [p.9 & p.22].
http://archive.org/details/TheSecretsOfTheFederalReserve
56   http://nl.wikipedia.org/wiki/Eustace_Mullins
57   Named after Senator Nelson Aldrich, the only non-banker of the club. Because Aldrich was a senator, the plan was named after him so that the public would not be suspicious.

operation with the New York bankers group around J.P. Morgan. The thinking behind the Democrats' plan was almost identical to the Aldrich plan but was received much more enthusiastically, although there still was a certain amount of criticism. This was a smart political move by the Wall Street bankers. The Federal Reserve Act contained many features that were needed to overcome the anticipated objections to a US central bank by the American public. The new entity would be a Federal Reserve System instead of a central bank. It would present itself as a collection of regional banks with a Federal Reserve Board to supervise them. The board would not be selected by bankers but by the President of the United States.

In December 1913, many senators assumed that the deciding vote on the Federal Reserve Act would not take place until the New Year. They left Congress to celebrate Christmas at home. Shortly before the holidays, however, a few controversial topics were scrapped from the bill, enabling the law to be passed in the last meeting before the Christmas holidays. The establishment of the Federal Reserve was a fact.

It was the most beautiful Christmas present Wall Street could have wished for. For the third time in US history, the monopoly on the printing of dollars was transferred from government to private banks. Not many politicians realized the far-reaching consequences this decision would have. Immediately after the introduction of the law, all US banks became compulsory shareholders of the Fed.

29.   Is the Fed really independent?

Officially, the Federal Reserve Bank of New York is only one of twelve regional Reserve Banks which make up the Federal Reserve System, together with the Board of Governors in Washington. But while the New York Fed serves only a geographically small area compared with the other Federal Reserve Banks, the New York Fed is the largest Reserve Bank in terms of assets and volume of activity. As a result, the New York Fed is far more important in the Fed system than all the other 11 regional Reserve Banks combined.

When the Federal Reserve Act was signed in 1913, the powerful New York banker Benjamin Strong[58] became president of the Federal Reserve Board (FRB) of New York up until his death in 1928. He drew a lot of power to himself, also within the Federal Open Market Committee (FOMC) where monetary policies were decided, and he often took decisions unilaterally.[59]

The FOMC, which happens to be based in New York, consists of seven governors who are chosen by the US President and five directors of the regional Federal Reserve banks. One of those five always comes from the New York Fed. So while the Federal Reserve presents itself as a normal central bank with twelve districts, the New York Fed is actually running the show. One hundred years after the Federal Reserve started, it is still unknown who precisely owns its shares[60] and how much they paid for them. But it is well known that shareholders are predominantly Wall Street banks.

---

58   Both were powerful bankers with connections in Europe. Strong was the vice president of the Banker's Trust of New York and friends with the Rothschilds, who in turn had control over the Bank of England. Warburg was a German immigrant who had close ties with the banking fraternity in Germany. He was also a partner of the Kuhn Loeb Bank in New York.

59   Murray N. Rothbard, *The Case Against the Fed*, p. 126.

http://www.lewrockwell.com/1970/01/murray-n-rothbard/the-case-against-the-fed/

60   http://www.federalreserve.gov/aboutthefed/section5.htm

After Strong's death, power remained centralized in New York. Up to this very day, only the New York Fed has a permanent seat on the FOMC and a permanent seat at the Bank for International Settlements, as the official US representation.[61] Furthermore, the New York Fed has the following unique responsibilities:

- Conducting open market operations;
- Intervening in foreign exchange markets (including gold);
- Storing monetary gold for foreign central banks, governments and international agencies;
- Implementing monetary policy and international operations.

At the outset, the founders of the Fed were wary of meddling by the government. For this reason, they decided that the presidents of the twelve regional Federal Reserve Banks (FRD) would be appointed by the participating banks.[62] This means that these are almost completely under the control of the banks.

A great deal of this information is still withheld from students of economics at most universities. Even most economists are not aware that the government does not own the shares of the Fed and that it is in fact Wall Street that controls the Fed instead of the other way around.

61   http://www.ny.frb.org/aboutthefed/fedpoint/fed22.html
62   Frederic S. Mishkin, *The Economics of Money, Banking and Financial Markets*, 2006, p. 314.

30.   When was the dollar system born?

Before World War II, the American economy was predominantly inward-looking. After the war, however, US companies realized the growth potential offered by new foreign markets and wanted to benefit from them. The British pound sterling, the world currency before World War I, had weakened significantly after it had left the gold standard in 1914. But this was only temporary, since a gold standard was re-introduced in 1925. Benjamin Strong, in his position as President of the New York Fed, pursued a successful policy of toppling the pound sterling from its position as the dominant international currency and replacing it with the dollar. The final blow to the pound sterling came when the currency was forced off the gold standard for a second time in September 1931.[63]

During both world wars, the dollar had become increasingly important outside of the US, and the US decided in early 1944 that it was time to take advantage of their anticipated victory. The Americans knew that upgrading the status of the dollar to that of a world currency would bring with it significant benefits.

Because several countries (including the UK) had made payments to the US in gold during World War II, and because the US had 'looted' quite a bit of gold, almost two-thirds of all financial gold reserves worldwide were at the disposal of the US at the end of World War. After President Roosevelt's executive order in 1933[64] which forbade individuals from owning gold, a significant amount of privately owned gold was confiscated, thereby considerably increasing US gold supplies as well. All of this gold could now be put to use to back the American dollar as the new world reserve currency.

---

63   In 1925, the US held 45% of all financial gold stock. (Official Monetary and Financial Institutions Forum, *Gold, the renmimbi and the multi reserve currency system*, 2013)

64   http://www.safehaven.com/article/14339/why-did-the-us-government-confiscate-gold-in-1933-and-can-it-happen-again-part-3

As the war drew to a close and after two and a half years of planning for postwar reconstruction, the US decided to present its proposal for a new international financial system. Finance ministers from 44 countries were invited to attend a conference in 1944 on the future of the world's financial system. This was the famous Bretton Woods conference, named after the forest surrounding the hotel where the conference took place. The idea was to build 'a system of international payments that would allow trade to be conducted without fear of sudden currency depreciation or wild fluctuations in exchange rates'. The US wanted to persuade other countries to support a move to a new monetary system built around the dollar instead of gold.

US real GDP and debt since 1945 _____

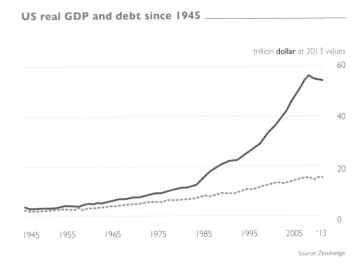

trillion **dollar** at 2013 values

Source: Zerohedge

31. What was decided at the Bretton Woods conference?

There were two plans on the drawing board for a new world currency. The economists John Maynard Keynes and Ernst Friedrich Schumacher proposed the creation of a new supranational currency, the Bancor. This idea was backed by the British, who resisted the idea of handing over the benefits of owning the world's reserve currency to the Americans.[65] The new Bancor was to be issued by the yet-to-be-formed International Monetary Fund. No single country would then enjoy the privileged position of owning the world's reserve currency.

The second plan, developed by Harry Dexter White, the chief international economist at the US Treasury during World War II, was a blueprint for the dollar to become the new world currency. As the main creditor nation, the US was eager to take on the role of the world's economic powerhouse. The American plan meant that all commodities would have to be traded in dollars, forcing all countries to buy dollars in order to be able to pay for them. The US would only need to turn on the printing press in order to be able to satisfy the permanent demand for dollars.

An important benefit of having its own currency as the world reserve currency is that the US could finance its trade deficits (when imports exceed exports) inexhaustibly by simply printing more dollars.[66] Wary of the repercussions of such an arrangement, Europe demanded that the dollars be exchangable for gold. After some discussion, it was agreed that countries would be allowed to exchange their excess dollars with the US against a fixed exchange rate of $ 35 for one ounce of gold. The US would

65 'The greatest blow to Britain next to the war', according to a senior official of the Bank of England (1944) in 'The Bretton Woods Sequel Will Flop' by Gideon Rachman, *The Financial Times*, 11 November 2008. http://www.relooney.info/o_New_3860.pdf

66 Costabile L. (2010), 'The International Circuit of Key Currencies and the Global Crisis: Is there Scope for Reform?' PERI Working paper series, number 220, 4-10.

in this way be restrained from building up too much debt. The US reluctantly accepted, secretly hoping that this agreement would be quickly forgotten.

Because of the overwhelming economic and military power of the US and the promise that the dollar would be backed by gold, in the end the participating countries agreed on White's plan. It would mark the start of the United States as the economic superpower for the rest of the 20th century.

32.   Why did Europe accept the dollar system?

The French in particular found it difficult to accept the fact
the US would be able to finance budget deficits by turning on
the printing press. They protested both in 1944 and thereafter
against the introduction of this dollar system. But France, like
many other European countries, needed financial help at the
end of World War II. It therefore accepted the Bretton Woods
plan and in return received millions of dollars in special aid. At
Bretton Woods, the US also proposed the Marshall Plan, which
was designed to help finance Europe after the devastations of the
war. Europeans did not know at that time that the Marshall Plan
also financed[67] the formation of the Central Intelligence Agency
(CIA). Ten percent of Marshall Plan funds was used to finance
CIA operations in European countries. This was arranged in
secret, without any knowledge or approval by the US Congress.

  General de Gaulle understood quite well that France and the
rest of the world would have to start financing US deficits by
buying up government bonds. Jacques Rueff, France's minister
of finance, de Gaulle's main adviser, remarked:

'If I had an agreement with my tailor that whatever money
I pay him he returns to me the very same day as a loan, I
would have no objection at all to ordering more suits from
him and my own balance of payments would then be in
deficit. Because of this situation, the United States could
pay off its balance of payments deficit in paper dollars.
(...) As the central banks received dollars, they used them
immediately to buy US Treasury Bills or certificates of
deposit in New York banks, thus returning the dollars to

67 https://www.cia.gov/library/center-for-the-study-of-intelligence/csi-
publications/csi-studies/studies/vol51no3/legacy-of-ashes-the-history-of-cia.html

their country of origin which thus recovered all the assets it had just paid out.'[68]

Other European countries were even more dependent on US financial help. After being saved by the Americans from Nazism, not many dared to question their newfound friendship with the US.

---

68 Metaphor used by Jacques Rueff to illustrate the privileged position the United States enjoys in the monetary system. *The Monetary Sin of the West*, Mac Millan, 1972

33.   For how long did the Bretton Woods system work?

Following the Bretton Woods conference, all national currencies became pegged to the dollar, which was linked to gold at a rate of $ 35 per ounce. The dollar was the official world's reserve currency and the anchor of the monetary system. The world now operated under a pseudo gold standard which economists call the 'gold exchange standard'.

Within a few years, American companies were buying up European companies with their overvalued dollars. The US was able to run huge budget deficits. When other countries warned that this could weaken the dollar, the US always promised to bring its deficits down. But this promise rang increasingly hollow amid sharply rising expenses of up to $ 100 billion from the Vietnam War.

The French had already clashed for more than a century with the US over a number of issues. Now they and other European countries became fearful that many more dollars were being created than could be backed by the amount of gold owned by the US.

In the latter part of the 1960s, France and some other countries started to exchange their surplus dollars for gold. President de Gaulle of France even gave a television address in which he explained the US dollar privilege:[69]

> 'The fact that many countries accept as a principle dollars being as good as gold for the payment of the differences existing for their advantage in the American balance of trade. This very fact leads Americans to get into debt, and get into debt for free at the expense of other countires at least in part with dollars only they are allowed to emit. Considering the serious consequences a crisis would have under such a system we think that measures must be taken in time to avoid it. We consider it necessary that

69   http://www.youtube.com/watch?v=EjRLsAzW6e4

international trade be established as it was before the great misfortunes of the world on an indisputable monetary base, one that does not bear the mark of any particular country. Which base? In truth, who can see, how one can have any real standard critereon, other than gold?'

France started by demanding gold in exchange for $ 150 million of their financial reserves and was planning to convert another $ 150 million. De Gaulle even sent the French navy to the US to transport the gold bars back home. Many other European countries followed. In this way, Germany's gold reserves increased from zero to 3,500 metric tonnes, Italy from just over 220 to 2,500 metric tonnes, France from almost 600 to 3,100 metric tonnes, and the Netherlands from 300 to almost 1,700 metric tonnes.

In early 1971, the Dutch Central Bank (DNB) successfully swapped nearly a billion dollars for gold. Paul Volcker, an important Treasury official who would later become Chairman of the Fed, was sent to Holland to try to change DNB President Jelle Zijlstra's mind.[70]

'You are rocking the boat', Volcker is said to have remarked. Zijlstra then replied, 'Well if this rocks the boat, then the boat is not very solid'.

70 http://marketupdate.nl/nieuws/economie/valutacrisis/dr-zijlstras-final-settlement-gold-as-the-monetary-cosmos-sun/
http://www.coinweek.com/commentary/opinion/former-central-banker-confirms-us-government-gold-price-suppression-efforts/

34. When did the US close its 'gold window'?

Between 1959 and 1971, the US lost over half of its gold reserves of over 20,000 metric tonnes. If this process had continued at the same rate, the US would have risked losing all its gold holdings within a few years' time. In the summer of 1971, President Richard Nixon refused a request by the Bank of England to exchange a few hundred million dollars for gold. After rejecting the British request, President Nixon asked his economic advisors for advice. Their verdict was short but sweet: 'Break the promise that the dollar can be exchanged for gold.'

Nixon followed their advice and on 15 August 1971 gave a live TV address announcing what he called his New Economic Policy. Nixon interrupted the most popular TV show in America, Bonanza, to announce that he would be introducing immediate wage and price controls, a 10% surtax on imports, and the closing of the gold window:[71]

> 'I have directed Secretary Connolly to suspend, temporarily, the convertibility of the American dollar into gold... In full cooperation with the IMF and those who trade with us, we will press for the necessary reforms to set up an urgently needed new international monetary system.'

As we now know, the closing of the gold window was not temporary, of course. And this book argues that we are still waiting for the new international monetary system promised by Nixon. But 1971 was a big financial reset when gold was repriced to \$ 38 per ounce (and then again to \$ 42 per ounce in 1973).

71   http://www.youtube.com/watch?v=iRzr1QU6K1o

35. How did the world react to Nixon's decision in 1971?

Technically speaking, America defaulted in August 1971, since the country could no longer fulfill the obligations agreed upon in Bretton Woods. But surprisingly, the Nixon shock created only a relatively short dollar panic in the world's financial markets.

Jacques Rueff warned in his book *The Monetary Sin of the West* (1971) about the long-term negative effects of inflationary policies. He explained that the use of a fiat dollar as a world reserve currency would cause worldwide inflation for years. The 'exorbitant privilege' allowed the US to run huge deficits but would be 'suicidal' for Western economies, he predicted. European countries were shocked when they later learned that the US had been planning to devalue the dollar even further. This led to panic buying of D-marks in the summer of 1972. In October 1978, the US dollar almost completely collapsed after a new wave of panic buying of D-marks and Swiss francs.

The fact that the dollar has survived as a reserve currency surprised many, including the Americans themselves. At first, the inflation caused by the printing of extra dollars was moderate, but later in the 1970s, inflation began to take off, leading to a severe recession in 1979 and 1980. It would take years of strong leadership by Fed Chairman Paul Volcker to tame inflation and make the dollar a 'strong' currency again. In June 1981, Volcker raised the federal funds rate to 20%. The shock therapy worked. Inflation collapsed from over 12% in 1980 to 1% in 1986, and the price of gold dived from $ 612 to $ 300. The dollar started to regain strength, especially when the greenback showed itself to be a safe-haven currency during the Mexican peso crisis in 1994 and the 1997 Asian crisis.

With the strengthening of the dollar, the need for a new international monetary system appeared to evaporate. However, this need is now more urgent than ever.

36. How important is the worldwide oil trade for the survival of the dollar?

After the short-lived dollar panic of 1971, the United States understood that a lack of trust in the dollar was going to be a problem. Clearly, some other backing for the dollar was urgently needed. Nixon and his Secretary of State, Henry Kissinger, feared a decline in the relative global demand of the US dollar. They needed to stabilize the dollar to maintain its global reserve currency status.

It was Henry Kissinger who came up with the idea[72] of asking Saudi Arabia to agree to only sell oil in dollars and to invest a portion of these dollars in US Treasuries.[73] The money that the US government received in this manner – known as petrodollars – would then be recycled back into the American economy.[74] This arrangement was to require a constant increase in the supply of dollars.

After a series of meetings, the Saudis accepted the American proposal. In return, Saudi Arabia was to receive any military protection needed for its royal family and its growing oil empire. The US also promised to help the country build a modern infrastructure (using American companies, of course).

The US had found a way to protect its economic hegemony.

The other OPEC countries followed, and by 1975 all of OPEC had agreed to sell their oil in dollars. Part of the deal was that they would all invest their surplus oil proceeds in US government debt securities in exchange for similar offers of funds by the US. The modernization of the Middle East could start. Dubai, a relatively small trading city in the United Arab Emirates with no running water up until 1961, was to become a worldwide trading hub in the ensuing 40 years.

---

72 http://www.thepeopleshistory.net/2013/06/understanding-petrodollar-means.html

73 *The hidden hand of American hegemony: Petrodollar recycling and international markets*, David E. Spiro (1999).

74 http://en.wikipedia.org/wiki/Petrodollar_recycling

It is no surprise that countries that chose to sell their oil for currencies other than the dollar were to meet serious opposition from the US. In 2000, Iraq converted all its oil transactions under the Oil for Food program to euros.[75] When the US invaded Iraq three years later, oil sales from this country switched from the euro back to dollars.

Iran created its own oil bourse in 2008.[76] It started selling oil in gold, euros, dollars and yen. Venezuela supported Iran's decision to sell oil for euros. Libya presented a threat to the petrodollar in 2010. Muammar Gaddafi wanted to create a pan-African currency called the gold dinar that could be used for their oil transactions. After the revolution in 2012, Libya continued to sell oil in dollars. Syria had switched to euros in 2006,[77] and the US has been seeking a regime change ever since.

In his 2005 book *Oil Currency War*, William R. Clarke explains that the US-UK decision to invade Iraq in 2003 was oil-driven. According to him, the petrodollar system was the driving force of US foreign policy.[78] It seems no coincidence that the Bush family has had close personal ties with the Saudi Royal Family since the 1970s. And even Alan Greenspan, who served as Fed Chairman for almost two decades, wrote in his memoirs:

I am saddened that it is politically inconvenient to acknowledge what everyone knows: the Iraq war is largely about oil.[79]

The only real challenge for the petrodollar trade would be if the BRICS – Brazil, Russia, India, China and South Africa – were to decide to drop the dollar in their trading transactions. It appears the days of the dollar as a world reserve currency are numbered.

75   http://www.rferl.org/content/article/1095057.html
76   http://en.wikipedia.org/wiki/Iranian_Oil_Bourse
77   http://www.informationclearinghouse.info/article11894.htm
78   http://www.zerohedge.com/news/2013-05-20/guest-post-coming-collapse-petrodollar-system
79   http://www.theguardian.com/world/2007/sep/16/iraq.iraqtimeline

37. What is the role of the IMF and World Bank in this dollar system?

The delegates of the Bretton Woods Conference also agreed to establish the International Monetary Fund (IMF), which would safeguard the world's financial system, and the International Bank for Reconstruction and Development (IBRD), which would act as a world investment bank. Both entities were pitched as bodies that would serve the interests of the world but were de facto controlled by the US When the neo-conservative Paul Wolfowitz was sworn in as President of the World Bank in 2006, it became quite obvious to many that fighting poverty in the world was not the World Bank's priority for the Americans.

John Perkins, chief economist for the Boston strategic consulting firm Chas. T. Main in the 1970s, wrote a book about his experiences advising Third World countries. He explains how the IMF and World Bank collaborated in the process of economic colonization of Third World countries on behalf of what he portrays as a 'cabal of corporations, banks, and the United States government'.[80] According to him, 'Third World countries were trapped into international debts they could not repay in order to get their resources handed over to US corporations, during an international financial IMF-led rescue operation.' The company Perkins worked for was a worldwide player in the utility industries at that time.

According to Perkins, the IMF and World Bank play a major role in supporting the dollar as a world reserve currency. During the Bretton Woods negotiations, the US also insisted that countries could only join the IMF after decoupling their currency from gold.[81] Once decoupled, the central banks, with some help by the Federal Reserve, were able to dump their enormous gold reserves.

80 http://www.amazon.com/John-Perkins/e/B000APETSY
81 Articles of Agreement, Article IV, Section 2(b): 'a member may not determine the value of its currency in terms of gold'.(https://www.imf.org/external/np/leg/sem/2004/cdmfl/eng/gianvi.pdf).

38. How transparent is the Fed?

According to the former Republican Congressman Ron Paul, the Federal Reserve is the chief culprit behind the current economic crisis. Because of its 'unchecked power to create endless amounts of money out of thin air', the Fed has caused one financial bubble after another. Paul also claims that by 'recklessly inflating the money supply, the Fed continues to distort interest rates and intentionally erodes the value of the dollar'. He calculates that the dollar has lost 'more than 96% of its value since the Fed's creation in 1913'. He also criticizes the strong culture of secrecy within the Fed organization.

The Fed's secrecy forced press agency Bloomberg to resort to the courts in order to obtain information about the Fed's rescue operation after the collapse of Lehman Brothers in the fall of 2008. On 5 December 2008, US banks had secretly received $ 1,200 billion in aid from the Fed,[82] while a full audit of the Federal Reserve later revealed that over $ 16 trillion[83] had been allocated to corporations and banks internationally, purportedly for 'financial assistance' during and after the 2008 financial crisis.

Since the 1990s, Ron Paul has been trying to force the secretive bank to become more transparent.[84] In 2010, Paul succeeded in including an amendment to a new Financial Reform Bill requiring that the Fed be audited. After reviewing the results of the audit in 2012, Senator Bernie Sanders remarked, 'The Federal Reserve must be reformed to serve the needs of working families, not just CEOs on Wall Street.'[85]

---

82 http://www.bloomberg.com/news/2011-11-28/secret-fed-loans-undisclosed-to-congress-gave-banks-13-billion-in-income.html

83 To give an indication of the enormity of this amount, $ 16 trillion ($ 16,000 billion) is the same amount as the total external debt of the US in 2012.

84 http://www.ronpaul.com/misc/congress/legislation/111th-congress-200910/audit-the-federal-reserve-hr-1207/

85 http://www.bloomberg.com/news/2011-11-28/secret-fed-loans-undisclosed-to-congress-gave-banks-13-billion-in-income.html

39. Have any Wall Street bankers gone to jail?

Bill Black is an associate professor of economics and law at the University of Missouri, Kansas City and author of *The Best Way to Rob a Bank is to Own One.* He is specialized in white-collar crime investigations and prosecutions.

Black claims that 'the U.S administration refuses to investigate and prosecute the elite bank fraudsters'. According to Black, 500 FBI agents working on white-collar crime cases were transferred to national security tasks immediately after the 9/11 terrorist attacks.[86]

The Department of Justice started a few dozen criminal investigations against Wall Street Bankers since 2000. But the only bankers sent to jail were those that had a conflict with one of the Wall Street banks or were punished for insider trading on their own account. Most of those cases were private frauds. In all other cases, a financial settlement was proposed to bankers and almost always accepted. The only exception my research showed was a criminal case against two ex-Merrill Lynch bankers who were convicted in a scheme involving a sham sale of Enron barges.[87]

US Attorney General Eric Holder, involved in many Wall Street criminal investigations, has suggested that pressure from the highest echelons was used to stop the prosecution of high-level bankers:[88]

---

86 http://neweconomicperspectives.org/2013/08/mueller-i-crippled-fbi-effort-v-white-collar-crime-my-successor-will-make-it-worse.html

87 James A. Brown, former head of the bank's asset lease and finance group who was convicted of lying and obstructing justice along with conspiracy and fraud in the barge deal, was sentenced to three years and 10 months in prison. He also had to undergo one more year under court supervision and pay $ 840,000 in fines. Daniel Bayly, the former global head of the investment banking division at Merrill Lynch, was sentenced to two years and six months in prison, a six-month supervised period and similar fines of $ 840,000. http://www.chron.com/business/enron/article/Former-Merrill-Lynch-executives-get-less-prison-1948896.php

88 http://www.washingtonpost.com/blogs/wonkblog/wp/2013/09/12/this-is-a-complete-list-of-wall-street-ceos-prosecuted-for-their-role-in-the-financial-crisis/

I am concerned that the size of some of these institutions becomes so large that it does become difficult for us to prosecute them when we are hit with indications that if you do prosecute, if you do bring a criminal charge, it will have a negative impact on the national economy, perhaps even the world economy.

No Wall Street CEO even came close to facing criminal charges. Angelo Mozilo, chief executive of Countrywide, was charged by the SEC with insider trading and securities fraud in 2009 for selling shares of his company while publicly proclaiming it was in good shape. But he was allowed to settle these civil charges with $ 67.5 million in fines and a lifetime ban from serving as an officer of a public company. The criminal investigation was dropped.

So Wall Street bankers have agreed to pay fines. Many fines. This is quite smart, because it is not the bankers themselves but their shareholders that will have to pay these bills.

On the next page you can find the results of my research (see Appendix II) on this subject. A study of hundreds of media reports shows that the total amount of fines and settlements paid by Wall Street banks between 2000 and 2013 to avoid prosecution, adds up to $ 100 billion. First some special notes:

* According to media reports at the end of 2013, US housing regulators were discussing details how to fine Bank of America over $ 6 billion for its role in misleading mortgage agencies during the housing boom, compared with the $ 4 billion to be paid by JPMorgan Chase & Co.[89]

If we add these extra settlements to the tally, the total amount of fines and settlements paid by Wall Street rises to well over $ 100 billion.

89   http://www.reuters.com/article/2013/10/20/us-bofa-settlement-idUSBRE 99J0AW20131020

Total amount of fines and settlements paid by Wall Street banks (in billion dollars)

Amount of Fines (in USD millions)

year	BoA	Citi	JPM	GS	WF	Other	Total bln $
2000	0	0	0	0	0	0	0
2001	58	0	1	1	0	0	60
2002	490	620	205	112	42	0	1.469
2003	0	134	179	10	0	0	322
2004	1.100	2.7	0	53	7	111	4.027
2005	462	2.100	4.700	40	37	0	7.293
2006	8	3	427	0	13	243	693
2007	30	15	1	3	7	0	55
2008	0	1.800	25	34	0	0	1.870
2009	33	4	76	65	42	686	906
2010	995	77	49	578	463	175	2.300
2011	9.300	286	453	20	1.400	0	11.400
2012	2.900	793	806	107	342	25.000	30.000
2013*	13.900	2.900	17.200	330	2.8	0	37.100
Totals:	29.300	11.400	24.000	1.400	5.900	26.200	97.600

BoA	Bank of America
Citi	Citigroup
JPM	JPMorgan Chase
GS	Goldman Sachs
WF	Wells Fargo

Chapter 4 – A Planet of Debt

Fiat money can only flee into one direction and that is gold.
– Alan Greenspan, former Chairman of the Federal
  Reserve Board (2010)

The process by which banks create money is so simple that the mind is repelled.
– John Kenneth Galbraith, economist (1975)

The first panacea for a mismanaged nation is inflation of the currency; the second is war. Both bring a temporary prosperity; both bring a permanent ruin. But both are the refuge of political and economic opportunists.
– Ernest Hemingway in Esquire (1935)

By this means government may secretly and unobserved, confiscate the wealth of the people, and not one man in a million will detect the theft.
– John Maynard Keynes on inflation (1920)

To destroy a bourgeois society, you must debauch its money.[90]
– Lenin

---

90   Quoted by Joseph Schumpeter in *Capitalism, Socialism, and Democracy* (New York: Harper & Row, 1950).

INTRO

The decoupling of gold and money made creating new money very simple. As a result, with the end of the gold exchange standard in the 1970s, an unprecedented credit bonanza was allowed to take off. In order to understand the build-up of debt, we must go back in time to 1981 when Fed Chairman Volcker was forced to raise interest rates to 20% in order to save the dollar's position as the world's reserve currency.

The dollar recovered as a result of Volcker's interest rate hike, and with inflation tamed, interest rates started to decrease sharply. The decline in interest rates after 1981 made it possible for governments to issue more debt. The same held true for companies and individuals. This period of unprecedented private debt build-up lasted until the start of the current credit crisis. Since then, the balance sheets of governments and central banks in particular have expanded significantly.

Countries with debt issued in their own currency cannot go bankrupt. They can always switch on the printing press to create as much money as is needed to pay off their debts. There is one drawback, however: when too much money is created, their economy can become paralyzed due to (hyper)inflation. At some point in time, even governments have to get rid of their debts. This will happen either through inflation, debt defaults or debt cancellations. Such monetary resets have been the solution many times in the past. It could well happen again.

40. When did the music stop?[91]

After over thirty years of falling interest rates, the period of unrestrained private build-up of debt came to an end with the start of the credit crisis. Falling real estate prices led to the first bank failures in 2007[92] in the US, after two years with no bank failures at all. Many American homeowners were no longer able to service their debts, and the banking system nearly collapsed completely. Between 2007 and the end of 2013, around 500 banks failed, most of them in the US. In order to prevent the house of cards from collapsing, central banks had to take on the role of lender of last resort.

In 2008, the US was confronted with the collapse of Wall Street banks, Ford and General Motors,[93] mortgage lenders Fannie Mae and Freddie Mac[94] and the world's largest insurer, AIG.[95] The then Secretary of the Treasury, ex-Goldman Sachs CEO Henry Paulson, proposed a large rescue operation on October 14th 2008, which was called the Troubled Asset Relief Program (TARP).

Politicians on Capitol Hill were pressured to accept a $ 700 billion rescue package to save financial institutions that had become icons in US society. Only Lehman Brothers was sacrificed, perhaps as punishment for being the only bank that had refused to join the 1998 rescue operation of the hedge fund Long-Term Capital Management (LTCM). Between 2008 and 2013, central banks worldwide created[96] over $ 10 trillion of new money to take

---

91 This is a reference to something Citigroup CEO Chuck Prince said in an interview with the Financial Times. When asked whether the boom in private equity buyouts would continue, he said 'When the music stops, in terms of liquidity, things will be complicated. But as long as the music is playing, you've got to get up and dance. We're still dancing.'
92 http://www.fdic.gov/bank/individual/failed/banklist.html
93 http://www.economist.com/node/13782942
94 http://www.theguardian.com/business/2008/sep/07/freddiemacfanniemae
95 http://www.dailywealth.com/506/aig-collapse-global-bank-run
96 http://viableopposition.blogspot.com/2013/07/the-worlds-central-banks-living-on.html

over bad loans from the private sector, to monetize debts and to stimulate the economy. The Fed balance sheet grew from $ 800 billion to almost $ 4,000 billion in just five years.

A 2013 study by James Felkerson revealed the Fed had committed a total of $ 29,616 billion dollars[97] in the wake on the Lehman crisis at the end of 2008.

Cumulative facility totals, in billions $[98]

Term Auction Facility	3,818
Central Bank Liquidity Swaps	10,057
Single Tranche Open Market Operation	855
Terms Securities Lending Facility and Term Options Program	2,005
Bear Stearns Bridge Loan	13
Maiden Lane I	29
Primary Dealer Credit Facility	8,950
Asset-Backed Commercial Paper Money Market Mutual Fund Liquidity Facility	218
Commercial Paper Funding Facility	737
Term Asset-Backed Securities Loan Facility	71
Agency Mortgage-Backed Security Purchase Program	1,850
AIG Revolving Credit Facility	140
AIG Securities Borrowing Facility	803
Maiden Lane II	20
Maiden Lane III	25
AIA/ ALICO	25
Totals	**$ 29,616**

97 Source: '$ 29,000,000,000,000: A Detailed Look at the Fed's Bail-out by Funding Facility and Recipient' by James Felkerson
98 http://www.economonitor.com/lrwray/2011/12/09/bernanke's-obfuscation-continues-the-fed's-29-trillion-bail-out-of-wall-street/#sthash.2VbAsJpo.dpuf

41. What has happened to the US national debt since the start of the credit crisis?

Sovereign debt in a number of countries has also increased significantly since the start of the credit crisis. In response to the economic downturn, fiscal deficits in many countries, including the US, have increased to sometimes over 10% of GDP.

Table 1.1

Year	US budget deficit/ GDP ratio
2008	$ 458 (-3,2%)
2009	$ 1,412 (-10,1%)
2010	$ 1,294 (-9,0%)
2011	$ 1,299 (-8,7%)
2012	$ 1,086 (-7,0%)
2013	$ 972 (-6,0%)

Source: http://www.whitehouse.gov/omb/budget/Historicals

The US national debt grew by $ 8 trillion in a five-year period to reach $ 17 trillion at the end of 2013. To put this into perspective, it took 169 years (from 1836 to 2005) for the first $ 8 trillion of national debt to accumulate.[99]

At the same time, mutual distrust between banks led to a virtual halt to interbank lending in the years after Lehman's collapse in 2008. In order to solve this problem, central banks have allowed commercial banks to borrow virtually unlimited amounts of money from them interest rates close to zero.

---

99 http://www.whitehouse.gov/omb/budget/Historicals

42. When does the size of fiscal deficits become dangerous?

Peter Bernholz, Emeritus Professor at the University of Basel in Switzerland, has analysed the twelve most severe episodes of hyperinflation. He concluded that all were caused by the financing of huge public budget deficits through money creation (QE). According to Bernholz, the tipping point at which hyperinflation will occur is when the government's deficit exceeds 40% of its expenditures. The US reached this level already in 2009, when revenues were $ 2,104 billion, while outlays were $ 3,517 billion.[100] The US government was apparently well aware of this risk, as this ratio has since come down to less than 35%.

Japan is also at risk of ending up with hyperinflation. The Japanese government's deficits now exceed 25% of its expenditures.[101] The gap between public spending and revenue was 9.1% of GDP in 2012. Debt service now accounts for almost half of government revenues.[102]

Year	Budget Deficit[105]	% of GDP
2008	10 tr. yen	-3.0%
2009	41 tr. yen	-8.8%
2010	40 tr. yen	-8.8%
2011	41 tr. yen	-8.7%

The Japanese government has to borrow heavily just to service its national debt. Since these deficits are almost completely internally financed (i.e., almost all buyers of Japanese government

100 http://www.whitehouse.gov/omb/budget/Historicals

101 http://www.tradingeconomics.com/japan/government-budget

102 http://www.economist.com/news/finance-and-economics/21577080-shinzo-abes-government-looks-likely-disappoint-fiscal-consolidation-dont

103 http://stats.oecd.org/Index.aspx?DatasetCode=SNA_TABLE12

bonds are Japanese investors),[104] Japan can pay off these debts in yens that it can create itself. The huge private savings in Japan are continuously being recycled into government bonds through national insurance companies and pension funds.[105] This system of financing its deficit is unsustainable because the savings rate has dropped to around 2% due to an aging population. Other structural problems are sluggish domestic demand and weak exports as well as the high cost of importing energy after Japan's nuclear plants were made idle in 2011. In 2013, the OECD warned that reducing debt must be a priority for Japan.[106] Japan intends to increase outlays by doubling its low sales tax to 10% by 2015.[107]

Japan goverment debt / GDP ratio (1885-2013)

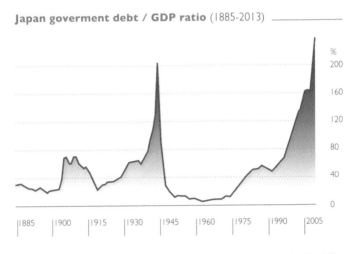

Source: Global Financial Data

104 The Japanese own 93% of their government's debt. In contrast, half of US Treasuries are held outside the US
105 One-fourth (25%) of Japanese bank deposits and almost 50% of bank assets are invested in Japanese government bonds. http://www.bloomberg.com/news/2012-06-05/japan-s-unsustainable-deficit-financing-model.html#disqus_thread
106 http://www.economist.com/news/finance-and-economics/21577080-shinzo-abes-government-looks-likely-disappoint-fiscal-consolidation-dont
107 http://www.bloomberg.com/news/2012-06-04/japan-s-debt-sustains-a-deflationary-depression.html

43. Didn't the credit crisis start much earlier in Japan?

Japan had a booming economy in the 1980s that ended in a fateful crash of the stock and real estate markets in the early 1990s. Since then, the Japanese economy has never fully recovered despite massive support operations. In 2013, the Japanese stock exchange Nikkei was still trading almost 70% lower than its record of almost 40,000 index points in 1989.

In order to save the Japanese financial system and to support the economy, Japan decided to turn on the printing presses of its central bank as well. Ongoing budget deficits have created a public debt of around 240% of GDP.[108] Despite extremely low interest rates, the debt service costs already amount to over 25% of tax revenues. If refinance rates were to increase to 3%, the costs would consume all public revenues. Although many banks have been supported by the government for years, they can still be categorized as 'zombie banks': they have access to just enough capital in order not to collapse but have too few liquid assets to issue loans. This is the situation we have been witnessing with banks in the West since the start of the crisis.

In March 2001, the Japanese central bank launched a new instrument to stimulate the economy and to avoid deflation: quantitative easing.[109] This surprised many because the Bank of Japan (BOJ) had for years rejected its use and, even as late as February 2001, declared that 'quantitative easing is not effective'.[110]

The BOJ has also maintained short-term interest rates at close to zero since 1999.

---

108 In 2012, one-third of total global national debt could be attributed to Japan, 23% to America and 32% to Europe as a whole.
109 http://www.imes.boj.or.jp/english/publication/edps/2002/02-E-03.pdf
110 http://www.imes.boj.or.jp/english/publication/mes/2001/me19-1-4.pdf

44.   Who is most aggressive in their QE policies, Japan or the US?

After the threefold disaster of an earthquake, tsunami and three meltdowns in Fukushima in March 2011, the Japanese government was forced to support the economy again and decided to use even more unorthodox monetary policies.[111] In April 2013, the BOJ announced that it would expand its QE programme by $ 1.4 trillion in the next two years.[112] This amount is twice as much as the Fed's aggressive QE programme (in relation to GDP), and this new programme could double the money supply over that period to 270 trillion yen ($ 2.8 trillion).

The biggest risk for the Japanese financial system now is a sell-off of government bonds. Japan Post Holdings, the largest financial institution in the world, has over 70% of its assets in Japanese government bonds (JGB). Since the Bank of Japan is trying to double its money base, this retirement fund has been liquidating $ 80 billion worth of JGBs because it wants to diversify its holdings.[113] Experts have started to warn openly of an imminent financial crisis in Japan.[114]

Ex-Soros adviser and member of the upper house of parliament Takeshi Fujimaki remarked in 2013:

> As we can see from the megabanks that are drastically
> reducing their JGB holdings, there are some company
> managers with a reasonable mind. The risk of a default

111   The destruction, excluding the nuclear ramifications, was initially estimated at only 4% of GDP, http://www.bloomberg.com/news/2012-06-03/strong-yen-belies-a-worrisome-japanese-economy.html

112   http://www.bloomberg.com/news/2012-06-03/strong-yen-belies-a-worrisome-japanese-economy.html

113   http://www.bloomberg.com/news/2012-06-03/strong-yen-belies-a-worrisome-japanese-economy.html

114   www.bloomberg.com/news/print/2013-08-01/ex-soros-adviser-fujimaki-says-tax-delay-fed-may-pop-jgb-bubble.html

is shifting from the private sector to the public as the BOJ splurges on JGBs. If we continue down this path, the credibility of the BOJ will be lost and the yen will plunge. It's impossible to avoid a default at this point.

45. Is China still financing the US?

Between 2000 and 2010, the Bank of China invested almost
$ 1 trillion dollars in US Treasuries. Because of its large trade
surplus, the Chinese national bank received more and more
dollars from companies trading with the US. But after the fall of
Lehman, it became increasingly clear that the US had abandoned
its strong dollar policy and was trying to deflate its dollar to
support American exports. According to statistics, China seems
to have stopped buying US Treasuries in 2010. In that year, Fed
president Timothy Geithner made a disastrous trip to China.
Reuters reported on his visit to Peking University:

> 'Chinese assets are very safe,' Geithner said in response to
> a question after a speech at Peking University, where he
> studied Chinese as a student in the 1980s. His answer drew
> loud laughter from his student audience, reflecting scepti-
> cism in China about the wisdom of a developing country
> accumulating a vast stockpile of US Treasuries instead of
> spending the money to raise living standards at home.[115]

Yu Yonding, a leading official of the Chinese central bank, made
matters even worse for the US when he remarked:[116]

> I wish to tell the US government: Don't be complacent and
> think there isn't any alternative for China to buy your bills
> and bonds. The euro is an alternative. And there are lots of
> raw materials we can still buy.

115 http://www.reuters.com/article/2009/06/01/usa-china-idUSPEK
14475620090601
116 http://seekingalpha.com/article/140796-multiple-warning-shots-from-china

From that moment on, the Chinese started to invest hundreds of billions of dollars per year in hard assets such as gold and other commodities.

After touring the Fed's Bureau of Public Debt in 2009, US Congressman Mark Kirk said:

> I am alarmed at how much debt was being bought by the US Federal Reserve due to absence of foreign investors. It would appear, quietly and with deference and politeness, that China has cancelled America's credit card, and I'm not sure too many people on Capitol Hill realize that this is now happening. There will come a time where the lack of Chinese participation may have a significant impact.[117]

Kirk also said that China was justified in its concerns about the returns from finance giants Fannie Mae and Freddie Mac, which were bailed out by the US government due to the financial crisis.

In November 2010, the Fed had to announce a second round of quantitative easing during which it would buy $ 600 billion of Treasuries over a period of eight months.[118]

QE3, a third round of quantitative easing, was announced in September 2012.[119] The Fed decided to launch a new $ 40 billion per month bond purchasing programme. Because of its open-ended nature, QE3 has earned the popular nickname of 'QE-Infinity'.

In December 2012, the FOMC announced an increase in the amount of open-ended purchases to $ 85 billion per month.[120] The programme was also intended to keep interest rates low.

---

117 http://www.google.com/hostednews/afp/article/ALeqM5i4estRSYeFBIIl9ke zxnP4jgoGZQ?hl=en

118 Censky, Annalyn (3 November 2010). 'QE2: Fed pulls the trigger'. CNNmoney. com. Retrieved 10 August 2011.

119 http://www.nasdaq.com/article/qe3-launched-the-ever-decreasing-effects-of-monetary-stimulus-cm174677

120 http://www.federalreserve.gov/newsevents/press/monetary/20121212a.htm

International investors would only be interested in buying US Treasuries with a much higher yield. Because of QE3, the Fed balance sheet has since increased by around $ 1 trillion a year.

46.   How large is China's credit growth?

According to John Mauldin, author of *The Endgame* and *Code Red*, China is 'even more addicted to money printing than the US or Japan'. It is hard to know how significant Chinese money growth is because Chinese statistics cannot be trusted completely. Even China's statistics bureau chief, Ma Jiantang, has admitted that his agency has publicized cases of manipulated economic numbers. Li Keqiang, who became premier in 2013, even said GDP figures were 'man-made' and 'for reference only'.[121] It is therefore difficult to get a full picture of the financial and economic developments in China.

Despite national financial reserves of almost $ 4,000 billion,[122] China has been confronted with its own debt crisis after the banking system's assets grew by $ 14 trillion between 2008 and 2013.[123] This is the same amount as the entire US banking system. China's credit to gross domestic product (GDP) ratio surged to more than 200% last year from just over 110% in 2008.[124]

Overstretched borrowers and local governments have migrated to off-balance-sheet structures within the 'shadow' banking system because so much money has been pumped into unprofitable projects. An Australian news report provides some details:

> According to the People's Bank of China (PBOC), trust loans rose 679% in the year ending December 2012, to 264 billion Yuan ($ 42 billion). High-interest rate trust loans now make up 16% of China's entire pool of financing. Trust loans, like payday loans in the US, have short maturities. Short-term

121 http://www.zerohedge.com/news/2013-09-25/china-beige-book-exposes-government-lies-conventional-wisdom-economic-expansion-chin
122 http://www.gfmag.com/component/content/article/119-economic-data/12374-international-reserves-by-countryhtml.html#axzz2gBaaCTuf
123 http://www.cnbc.com/id/100966830
124 http://www.cnbc.com/id/100840536

trust loans amount to an estimated 50% of Chinese GDP, so liquidity crises can quickly spiral into solvency crises. Local governments are big trust loan borrowers. When one bank fears another bank might have exposure to dodgy trust companies, it now demands a high interest rate to compensate for risk. The Shanghai Interbank Offered Rate (SHIBOR) – the rate banks charge each other for loans – spiked from 3% to 13% in a matter of weeks early 2013.[125]

Estimates by UBS put the size of the nation's so-called shadow banking system at $ 3.4 trillion, which is equal to 45% of gross domestic product.[126] In Wenzhou, almost 90% of families and 60% of companies participate in the informal market for loans, according to a 2011 survey by the People's Bank of China.

Through this combination of factors, a dangerous debt cocktail has developed in China as well. China's sovereign wealth fund was needed to help recapitalize some national banks, which had to write off hundreds of billions of yuan in bad loans. Because of this, credit rating agency Moody's issued a stern warning on China's pyramid bank recapitalizations in 2010.[127] Ratings agency Fitch has warned that the scale of credit in the economy was so extreme that China would find it difficult to grow its way out of the excesses.[128]

In 2004, the central bank of China (PBoC) rescued some banks as well by injecting a tenth of its reserves into two of the big four state-owned banks, China Construction Bank (CCB)

125 http://www.moneymorning.com.au/20130626/chinas-growth-story-ends-with-a-whimper.html

126 http://www.businessweek.com/articles/2013-04-25/regulating-chinas-shadow-banking-system-isnt-easy

127 http://www.zerohedge.com/article/moodys-issues-stern-warning-chinas-pyramid-bank-recapitalization-scheme-has-cic-entered-fund

128 http://www.scmp.com/business/banking-finance/article/1139307/fitch-warns-over-chinas-local-government-debt

and Bank of China (BOC).[129] The central bank's balance sheet was used in a manner similar to Japan, the US and Europe in recent years.

The French bank Société Générale concluded in a 2011 study:[130]

> We are considerably concerned about the rising financial leverage in the Chinese system, in combination with a forthcoming peak in the Chinese labour force and a rapid rise in real estate prices.

Goldman Sachs concluded:

> There is tremendous confidence in the ability and the willingness of the Chinese Communist party to bail everyone out, but as the system gets bigger and bigger, there are more questions about how feasible that is.[131]

Just as in Japan, China is confronting a rapidly aging population. This will result in a declining population after 2030 and could well end the country's phenomenal growth story in the coming decades.

129 http://www.economist.com/node/2338716
130 http://www.ibtimes.com/chinas-local-government-debt-crisis-though-heavily-leveraged-linked-shadow-banks-provincial-1442176
131 http://www.cnbc.com/id/100966830

47.   Is the renminbi ready to replace the dollar?

According to a study by the Official Monetary and Financial Institutions Forum (OMFIF) entitled *Gold, the Renminbi and the Multi-Currency Reserve System* (2013),[132] the Chinese realize that their currency will not be able to compete with the dollar before 2020 because it will take some time for the renminbi to become fully convertible. But the renminbi could well become a co-world reserve currency in the years to come. China has publicly stated that it is dissatisfied with the present dollar-orientated system.

China is the only one of the world's six largest economies that does not have a reserve currency status, but the OMFIF report argues that it will take many years before the renminbi will mount a credible challenge to the dollar:

> The world is headed towards the uncharted waters of a durable multi-currency reserve system, where the dollar will share its pivotal role with a range of other currencies, including the renminbi. China will rise as the US wanes, but this rebalancing will occur gradually rather than abruptly, and setbacks and perturbations are likely along the way.

Between 2002 and 2012, the Chinese experienced the dangers of being dependent on the dollar and/or the euro. As a result, the Chinese Communist Party has decided to make the renminbi a true international trading currency. China started to sign bilateral renminbi trading agreements with dozens of countries between 2010 and 2014.

In 2012, China outlined a route map for full renminbi internationalization in the next decade. The Communist Party leadership is well aware of the risks of a change in monetary policy

132 http://www.omfif.org/media/in-the-press/2013/gold-the-renminbi-and-the-multi-currency-reserve-system/

because the previous Nationalist government was weakened and ultimately had to withdraw from mainland China primarily because they had lost control of the monetary system in the 1940s.

China's total debt / GDP ratio (2002-2012)

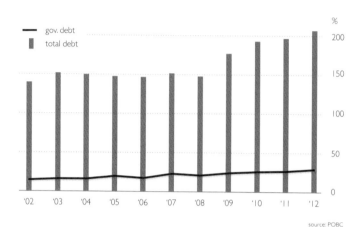

source: POBC

48. So China is fearful of making too sudden monetary changes?

The older generation of Chinese communist leaders still remember how they managed to grab power because of the monetary problems between 1937 and 1949. Their main goal is to avoid social unrest such as the period of hyperinflation China experienced after World War II.

Until 1927, China had a free banking system based on a silver standard. When Chiang Kai-shek's Nationalist Party came to power in 1927, he wanted to eliminate free banking in China. The nationalists used bank loans instead of taxation to finance their programmes. When Manchuria was lost to the Japanese in 1931, the economy took a hit and government bonds lost half of their value.[133] The Japanese invaders robbed some 6,600 tonnes of gold from Nanking, which was then the capital.

Due to a tripling of the price of silver, massive amounts of silver flowed out of China to the US in the 1930s. This resulted in a deep recession in China, with GDP declining by 26% in 1934 when the government imposed foreign-exchange controls to limit the silver exports. The Nationalists then issued the Savings Bank Law which required each bank to buy government bonds for a total of 25% of their deposits. The Bank of China, the largest private bank, decided to sell its government bonds that year. In order to prevent the bond market from collapsing, the Nationalists began a propaganda campaign against the bankers. They blamed China's economic woes on private bankers who placed their profits above the public interest.

In 1935, the government seized control of the Bank of China and other banks. This ended private banking in China. The Central Bank of China announced the Currency Decree at the end of 1935. The silver standard was replaced by a fiat currency, and the Nationalist government started to monetize its debt. In

133 The History of China's Internal Loan Issues, 1980.

addition, citizens who owned silver were ordered to exchange it for the new currency.[134] Economists around the world applauded this development, seeing it as a step toward a modern banking system. Massive monetary inflation occurred from July 1937 to September 1945 to fund the war against Japan. An estimated 60% percent of the annual expenditures were covered by newly printed money.

The national printing presses could not keep up with demand, so Chinese bank notes had to be flown in over the Himalayas from England.[135] A period of hyperinflation started in 1947 after the civil war between the Nationalist government and Communist forces led by Mao Zedong had restarted. With hyperinflation destroying people's savings, the ensuing sharp rise in poverty led to strong support for the communists, just as in Germany where the economic hardships following hyperinflation led to support for the Nazis. Once the Nationalists realized they were going to lose power, Chiang Kai-shek's army withdrew to Taiwan in late 1949, taking a secret shipment of 115 tonnes of gold with them.[136] Soon a new Chinese yuan replaced the old depreciated yuan at a conversion rate of three million to one.[137] Between 1931 and 1949 China lost almost all its gold and became 'hostage to paper money'.[138]

China clearly understands the current economic risks. This is why the Chinese are trying to hedge by buying massive amounts of gold. I will delve into this in more detail in a later chapter.

134 New Monetary System of China, 1936.

135 China's Wartime Finance and Inflation: 1937-1945.

136 *The Archives of Gold*, 2010, statement of Dr Wu Sing-yung.

137 Richard M. Ebeling, *The Great Chinese Inflation*.

138 http://therealasset.co.uk/nationalist-china-gold/

49.   How big is Europe's debt problem?

The ECB has also been very active in supporting the economies of member states, since 2008. But with the outbreak of the Greek crisis in 2010 and problems with rapidly rising interest rates in Portugal, Spain and Italy, the ECB has accelerated the expansion of its balance sheet, buying up government bonds. According to its own treaty, the ECB is not allowed to purchase government bonds directly, so the purchases totaling some € 1 trillion were made indirectly via commercial banks under the banner of long-term refinancing operations (LTRO).

The money created by the ECB in their LTRO was first lent out to commercial banks. These banks then bought the national government bonds of their own country to help bring interest rates down and to support their national economies. These newly bought bonds could then be used again as collateral for a new ECB LTRO-loan.

According to Bundesbank board member Carl-Ludwig Thiele, the ECB bond purchases were a 'violation of the Maastricht Treaty, against the prohibition of monetary financing, that a central bank should not give credit to a state'.[139] His comments are 180 degrees opposed to the official Bundesbank line. The German central bank argued that the bond purchases made until 2012 did not violate the prohibition of monetary financing.

Thiele remarked that the ECB only bought the government bonds of Spain and Italy to lower borrowing costs for Madrid and Rome. He explained:

The idea that the current crisis could be overcome by turning on the printing press should finally be discarded.

139 https://mninews.marketnews.com/index.php/bbk-thiele-current-ecb-government-bond-buys-violate-treaty?q=content/bbk-thiele-current-ecb-government-bond-buys-violate-treaty

This would only endanger the most important basis for a stable currency.

The Bank of England (BOE) has also purchased UK government bonds (gilts) to support the economy, especially from financial institutions such as banks, insurance companies and pension funds. The total amount of money created during its QE programme from 2010 to 2014 was around £375 billion ($ 598 billion). The BOE has stated that it will not buy more than 70% of any issue of government debt.[140]

But compared with Japan, where the size of QE is double the size of the American programme (relative to GDP), money printing has been slowing down in Europe between 2012 and 2014.

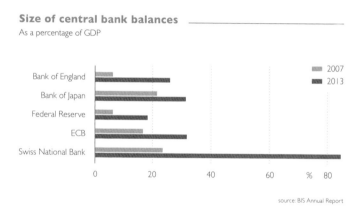

Size of central bank balances
As a percentage of GDP

source: BIS Annual Report

140 http://www.bbc.co.uk/news/business-16538773

50.   Is Switzerland still a monetary safe haven?

As a result of all the monetary madness after the outbreak of the financial crisis in 2008, more and more money started to flee to Switzerland. This caused the Swiss franc to gain in value, which had a substantial negative impact on Swiss exports and tourism. To avoid further harm, the Swiss National Bank (SNB) pegged the Swiss franc to the euro at a value of 1.20 euro.

By creating Swiss francs out of thin air and using them to buy euros and other currencies, the SNB has weakened the Swiss franc and strengthened other currencies. The international currencies bought during this operation ended up on the balance sheet of the SNB, which quadrupled in size between 2008 and 2013.

At the end of 2013, the SNB had the most holdings relative to GDP (85%) of any major industrialized country. This compares to the Federal Reserve's holdings of 20% of US GDP and the ECB's assets worth 30% of Eurozone GDP.[141]

The Swiss central bank required commercial banks to increase their capital to around 20% of their balance sheets, instead of the international norm of 7%.[142] The sheer size of the balance sheets of Credit Suisse and UBS formed a threat to the Swiss economy as a whole, as a bailout would have bankrupted the country.[143]

141 http://online.wsj.com/article/SB10001424127887323689604578221470075341686.html
142 Switzerland has abandoned the gold standard in order to join the International Monetary Fund in 1992. The IMF forbids countries to back their currency by gold.
143 This phenomenon is also frequently called 'too big to bail (out)': a variation on too big to fail, whereby a bank has become too important for the economy because of its size and thus has to be saved. In early 2009, the Dutch government found out that ING Bank was far too big to be bailed out. The total balance of ING of € 1,300 billion turned out to be twice the size of Dutch GDP.

51. What is happening in the so-called currency wars?

In 2010, the Brazilian minister of finance Guido Mantega warned of a 'currency war', pointing to a trend in which a number of central banks' monetary policies and foreign exchange interventions were leading to a vicious circle of competitive devaluations.[144] Most of the major G-20 economies have now resorted to devaluing their currency to deflate their way out of economic misery. By devaluing its currency, a country attempts to gain a competitive advantage because it stimulates its exports and tourism. This has led to a worldwide collective debasement of currencies the likes of which we have not seen before in monetary history.

Other emerging market economies have complained about the easy money policies in many developed countries. They have called the 'currency wars' the modern-day equivalent of the 'beggar-thy-neighbour'[145] policies of the 1930s.[146]

In early 2013, the first deputy chairman of the Central Bank of Russia, Aleksey Ulyukaev, warned that 'We are now on the

144 http://www.zerohedge.com/news/2013-08-25/three-years-after-warning-currency-war-brazil-goes-all

145 'Beggar-thy-neighbor policies are those that seek to increase domestic economic welfare at the expense of other countries' welfare. What might be called the classic case of beggar-thy-neighbor policies occurs when one country devalues its currency in order to boost its domestic output and employment but, by so doing, shifts the output and employment problem onto other countries. This occurred in the 1930s when, faced with a worldwide recession, countries sought to increase their own output and employment by devaluing their currencies, a policy that would boost domestic output by reducing the demand for imports and increasing the demand for exports. This exacerbated the recession in other countries, however, and invited the response of devaluations by other countries and countries became locked into a series of competitive devaluations... The solution to the use of beggar-thy-neighbor policies in the 1930s was found in the international policy coordination instituted under the auspices of the Bretton Woods system.' http://world- economics.org/40-beggar-thy-neighbor-policies.html

146 http://emlab.berkeley.edu/~eichengr/curr_war_JPM_2013.pdf

threshold of a very serious, I think, confrontational action, which is called, maybe excessively emotionally, currency wars.'[147]

In reaction to this criticism, Fed Chairman Ben Bernanke remarked that a return to solid growth in the US, Europe and Japan would ultimately benefit smaller countries as well:

> Because stronger growth in each economy confers beneficial spillovers to trading partners, these policies are not 'beggar-thy-neighbour' but rather are positive-sum, 'enrich-thy-neighbour'.[148]

He also argued that almost all G-7 industrialized countries have taken on similar easy monetary policy stances, which have led to small movements in foreign exchange (forex) markets:

> Because monetary policy is accommodative in the great majority of advanced industrial economies, one would not expect large and persistent changes in the configuration of exchange rates among these countries.

As a consequence, most of the currencies involved have stayed on a par with each other. To the general public, the dollar, the British pound, the euro and the Swiss franc all seem to have kept their value. But this is only with respect to each other. Because of this 'debasement of currencies', the smart money has started to flee towards commodities and other hard assets.

147 http://rt.com/business/news/currency-war-ulyukaev-japan-104/
148 http://www.marketwatch.com/story/bernanke-qe-is-an-enhance-thy-neighbor-policy-2013-03-25/print?guid=67E7F1BE-955E-11E2-9D5E-002128040CF6

52.   Can we grow our way out of this debt?

We have now arrived at the point where it is not the banks but the countries themselves that are in serious financial trouble. After years of enormous budget deficits, countries such as Greece and Portugal are now in need of financial assistance themselves. These deficits could be lowered in one of two ways: by cutting expenditures or raising taxes. Both options are politically unfeasible and would worsen the recession these countries are experiencing. In order to stimulate their economies, many countries have decided to allow large budget deficits and rising sovereign debt, as we have seen.

In the eighteen most important countries belonging to the OECD (the Organisation for Economic Co-operation and Development), the total amount of public and private debt (relative to GDP) grew from 160% in 1980 to 321% in 2011. This amassing of debt has not caused any problems, since the interest rate over the same period fell from over 20% in 1980 to almost 0% after the credit crisis. National debts increased by 425% on average and have risen in many countries to almost 100% of their GDP.[149]

The largest expansion of debt (600%) can be seen among consumers, which is mainly the result of higher mortgages. In the Eurozone, the Netherlands heads the list of highest mortgage debt per inhabitant. The total amount of Dutch debt has grown from € 550 billion in 1980 to at least € 4 trillion in 2010.[150] Over half of this is attributable to the financial sector. The government, companies and private investors have borrowed the other half. Only in countries with a conservative housing market, such as Germany, Italy and Greece, total debt by homeowners on average is less than 70% of GDP.

---

149 It is noticeable that in Greece during that period, the increase in debt amounted to only 70% of GDP (Boston Consulting Group, 2012).
150 *The Real Effects of Debt*, Bank for International Settlements (BIS), August 2011; Cecchetti, Moharty & Zampolli, Sept 2011.

Many countries are ill prepared to provide for the coming wave of pensioners. Most countries have set aside little money for the rising number of pensioners. In France, for instance, only € 2,300 per inhabitant has been reserved in the private pension system, while in the Netherlands this reserve is € 63,000. Germany has set aside only € 4,850 per inhabitant, lagging considerably behind the US (€ 42,000).[151]

According to an assessment by the Boston Consulting Group, the excess of debt in the EU amounts to $ 6,000 billion and $ 11,000 billion in the US These debts need to be restructured before a sustainable recovery can be achieved.

So the idea that we can 'grow our way back' out of debt seems a little naive. If history has taught us anything, it is that this would only work in a situation of strong economic growth. The UK managed to do so after its wars against Napoleon. Many Western countries after World War II also succeeded in growing themselves out of their debts. The debts caused by the 1997 Asian crisis were also resolved in this manner. In all these cases, the economy was able to re-launch high levels of growth because these countries were in an earlier phase of their economic life cycle.

151 This is shown in research conducted by Towers Watson (February 2011) as published in Fondsnieuws (Fund News).

53.   How can we get rid of our debts?

The current solution of 'parking' debts onto the balance sheets of central banks is an interim solution. Although limits do not apply to the balance of a central bank and debts could be 'parked' there for an unlimited amount of time in theory, in the end, debts will need to be restructured before the general public starts to lose faith in the value of the currency. Countries have a number of options to tackle their mountains of debt:

1) Defaulting - In the last century, the Russians experienced this three times, as have the Germans. Only Switzerland has never taken this route. Bankruptcy is the most expensive way of getting rid of debts. The financier is forced to write off the total amount as a loss on his capital.

2) Inflating - By turning on the printing presses and by inducing inflation, national debts can be 'inflated' away. Foreign holders of national bonds will get their money back, but calculated in purchasing power terms, they will lose a lot. This is the path of least resistance which many countries are choosing at this moment. By creating strong inflation, debt levels in relation to GDP will decline.

3) Raising taxes - By increasing revenue, countries can start to pay off debts. This is, however, a precarious strategy when economic growth is weak or negative, as is the case in most industrialized countries. In a democratic system, the decision to raise taxes is tantamount to political suicide. All the American presidents over the last twenty years had promised to lower taxes during their election campaign. This is why politicians prefer a simpler route – using the balance sheets of the central bank.

The IMF is studying 'more drastic measures and recommends a series of escalating income and consumption tax increases culminating in the direct confiscation of assets'.[152] In 2012, it was suggested in Germany that the rich should be required to invest a one-off 15% of their capital in special national bonds. Virtually all rich people have amassed their capital largely as a result of the fact that their possessions have increased in value due to credit becoming cheaper and cheaper. Especially the housing booms have been a substantial source of wealth for the baby-boom generation.

2011 Deficit as percentage of Goverment Expenditures ____

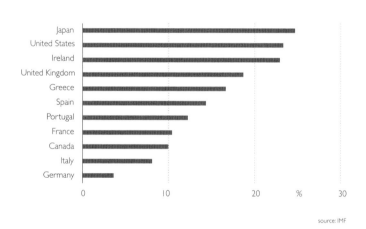

source: IMF

152 http://www.forbes.com/sites/billfrezza/2013/10/15/the-international-monetary-fund-lays-the-groundwork-for-global-wealth-confiscation/

54. How have debt cancellations worked before?

In both the Jewish and Christian traditions, one can find a so-called 'year of Jubilee', a year of universal pardon. In Hebrew Mosaic law, each fiftieth year was to be celebrated as a jubilee year when land would be returned to its former owners, slaves would be set free and debts would be remitted. The French finance minister Abbe Terray, who lived in the 18th century, thought governments should default once every hundred years in order to restore balance.[153]

Most countries simply pretend they will repay their debts. But if history is any guide, when the mountain of debt becomes too large, a default will occur. The debt then has to be restructured or refinanced. This has happened again and again. The US has defaulted in different ways three times in the last 220 years – in 1790, 1933 and 1971 – and borrowed more after each default. Switzerland is the only country that has always repaid its creditors. The Netherlands was once negligent in meeting payment commitments after the Napoleonic wars in 1802. And the US once actually reimbursed all of its debt entirely, in January 1835.[154] The government promptly began building up debt once again in the following year (the debt on 1 January 1836 was $ 37,000).

In *This Time is Different: Eight Centuries of Financial Folly* (2009), the most important[155] study on the history of financial crises, Carmen M. Reinhart and Kenneth S. Rogoff argue:

> Spain's defaults establish a record that remains as yet unbroken. Spain managed to default seven times in the nineteenth century alone after having defaulted six times in the preceding three centuries. With its later string of

153 http://scholar.harvard.edu/files/this_time_is_different_short.pdf
154 http://www.publicdebt.treas.gov/history/1800.htm
155 *The History of Financial Crisis* by Charles P. Kindleberger is another interesting book on this topic.

nineteenth-century defaults, Spain took the mantle for most defaults from France, which had abrogated its debt obligations on nine occasions between 1500 and 1800… Austria and Portugal defaulted only once in the period up to 1800, but then each defaulted a handful of times during the nineteenth century, and in the case of Austria into the twentieth century. Edward III, of Britain, defaulted on debt to Italian lenders in 1340, after a failed invasion of France that set off the Hundred Years' War… Starting in the nineteenth century, the combination of the development of international capital markets together with the emergence of a number of new nation states, led to an explosion in international defaults…and rescheduling episodes in Africa, Europe and Latin America. We include debt reschedulings, which the international finance theory literature rightly categorizes as negotiated partial defaults.[156]

The growth penalty arising from debt defaults are sometimes short-lived. The economies of Iceland, Argentina, Uruguay, Russia and Indonesia all did quite well after their respective defaults in recent history.[157]

156 http://scholar.harvard.edu/files/this_time_is_different_short.pdf
157 http://www.economist.com/blogs/dailychart/2011/06/sovereign-defaults-and-gdp

55. Possible debt cancellation scenarios

In 2013, US Congressman Alan Grayson proposed that the Fed could cancel the Treasury debt it owns.[158] The Fed owned roughly $2 trillion out of a total of $17 trillion of Treasury debts.[159]

According to Grayson:

> The debt held on the balance sheet of the Federal Reserve can be canceled without any significant consequence, because it is a bookkeeping artifact corresponding to the money supply. In essence, the government owes this money to itself. If I owe money to myself, I can cancel that debt at will and without consequence, essentially taking it out of my left pocket and putting it in my right pocket. A cancellation of this part of the US debt would give the government substantial room under the debt ceiling to manage its finances. This idea was put forward a few years ago not by me, or by a member of my party, but by Republican Representative Ron Paul. While canceling the Treasury debt held on the Federal Reserve balance sheet might be considered unorthodox, it is no more unorthodox than the quantitative easing that has added much of this debt to the Fed's balance sheet.[160]

Former BBC Chairman and Goldman Sachs partner Gavyn Davies wrote an important article about this subject in the

158 According to Zerohedge.com, similar proposals have been debated by economist Abba Lerner in the 1940s on 'functional finance' and the role of fiat money. More recently, the Modern Monetary Theorists have reawakened Lerner's ideas.'
159 http://www.zerohedge.com/contributed/2013-10-12/fed-could-simply-cancel-2-trillion-government-debt
160 Paul introduced a bill in 2011 which would have led to the cancellation of $1.6 trillion in federal debt held by the Fed. http://thehill.com/blogs/floor-action/house/174953-rep-paul-introduces-bill-to-cancel-public-debt-held-by-the-fed

Financial Times, 14 October 2013, entitled 'Will central banks cancel government debt?'[161]

One radical option now being discussed is to cancel (or, in polite language, 'restructure') part of the government debt that has been acquired by the central banks as a consequence of quantitative easing (QE). After all, the government and the central bank are both firmly within the public sector, so a consolidated public sector balance sheet would net this debt out entirely. This option has always been viewed as extremely dangerous on inflationary grounds, and has never been publicly discussed by senior central bankers, as far as I am aware. However, Adair Turner, the chairman of the UK Financial Services Agency, and reportedly a candidate to become the next governor of the Bank of England, made a speech last week that said more unorthodox options, including 'further integration of different aspects of policy', might need to be considered in the UK. Two separate journalists (Robert Peston of the BBC and Simon Jenkins of The Guardian) said that Lord Turner's 'private view' is that some part of the Bank's gilts holdings might be cancelled in order to boost the economy. ... Why is this such a radical idea? No one in the private sector would lose out from the cancellation of these bonds, which have already been purchased at market prices by the central bank in exchange for cash. The loser, however, would be the central bank itself, which would instantly wipe out its capital base if such a course were followed. The crucial question is whether this matters and, if so, how. In order to understand this, we need to ask ourselves why governments finance their deficits through the issuance of bonds in the first place, rather than just asking the

161 http://blogs.ft.com/gavyndavies/2012/10/14/will-central-banks-cancel-government-debt/?Authorised=false

central bank to print money, which would not add to public debt. Ultimately, the answer is the fear of inflation. When it runs a budget deficit, the government injects demand into the economy. By selling bonds to cover the deficit, it absorbs private savings, leaving less to be used to finance private investment. Another way of looking at this is that it raises interest rates by selling the bonds. Furthermore the private sector recognizes that the bonds will one day need to be redeemed, so the expected burden of taxation in the future rises. This reduces private expenditure today. Let us call this combination of factors the 'restraining effect' of bond sales. All of this is changed if the government does not sell bonds to finance the budget deficit, but asks the central bank to print money instead. In that case, there is no absorption of private savings, no tendency for interest rates to rise, and no expected burden of future taxation. The restraining effect does not apply. Obviously, for any given budget deficit, this is likely to be much more expansionary (and potentially inflationary) than bond finance. This is not, however, what has happened so far under QE. Fiscal policy, in theory at least, is set separately by the government, and the budget deficit is covered by selling bonds. The central bank then comes along and buys some of these bonds, in order to reduce long-term interest rates. It views this, purely and simply, as an unconventional arm of monetary policy. The bonds are explicitly intended to be parked only temporarily at the central bank, and they will be sold back into the private sector when monetary policy needs to be tightened. Therefore, in the long term, the amount of government debt held by the public is not reduced by QE, and all of the restraining effects of the bond sales in the long run will still occur. The government's long-run fiscal arithmetic is not impacted. Note that QE under these conditions does not directly affect the wealth or expected income of the private sector. From the private sector's viewpoint, all that happens is they hold more liquid assets (especially commercial bank deposits at the central bank), and fewer illiquid assets (i.e. government bonds). Because this is just a temporary asset swap, it may impact the level of bond yields, but otherwise its economic effects may be rather limited. Now consider what would happen if the bonds held by the central bank were cancelled, instead of being one day sold back into the private sector. Under this approach, the long-run restraining effect of bond sales would also be cancelled, so there should be an immediate stimulatory effect on nominal demand in the economy. If done without amending the path for the budget deficit itself, this would increase the expansionary effects of past deficits on nominal demand, and would also reduce the outstanding burden of public debt associated with such deficits. The central banks have now purchased so much government debt that the effects of such an action could be large. This is the situation in the UK, where the Bank of England holds 25 per cent of all outstanding government debt: Furthermore, the effects would be increased even more if, instead of just cancelling past debt, the central bank were to co-operate with the government, agreeing to directly finance an increase in the budget deficit by printing money. We would then be genuinely in the world of 'helicopter money', with no pretense of separation between fiscal and monetary policy. Outside of wartime, developed economies have not been normally been willing to contemplate any such actions. The potential inflationary consequences, which are in fact signalled by the elimination of central bank capital which this strategy involves, have always been considered too dangerous to unleash. For me, that remains the case. But others are more worried about deflation than inflation. This genie might soon be leaving the bottle.'

Total assets central banks

In trillions of respective currency units

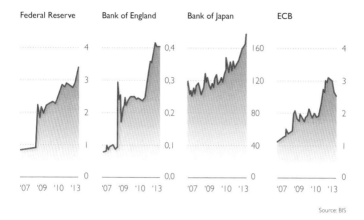

Federal Reserve   Bank of England   Bank of Japan   ECB

Source: BIS

56.   When do things go wrong?

Reinhart and Rogoff[162] demonstrate that when the national debt rises to over 90% of GDP, this tends to slow future economic growth.[163] They also prove that episodes where debt is above 90% have been quite rare in history. According to their study, a number of countries have never had debt above that level.

After World War II, US debt represented 120% of GDP. In most other countries debts reached similar record levels at that time.[164]

According to Reinhart and Rogoff, other examples of high-debt episodes are:

– The 1920s in France and Belgium
– Greece in the 1930s and 1990s to the present
– Ireland in the 1980s
– Italy in the 1990s,
– Spain around 1900
– UK in the interwar period and prior to the 1860s
– Japan since 2000

They also point out that the cumulative increase in public debt in the three years following a banking crisis is on average 186%. This explains why public debt in many advanced countries (the US, Japan, the UK) has increased strongly in recent years and reached or even crossed the 90% level.

While emerging markets have often been associated with defaults, Reinhart and Rogoff demonstrate that advanced economies have had their own share of default episodes. The high number of sovereign defaults often coincides with a sharp rise in the number of countries going through banking crises.

---

162 http://www.newyorker.com/online/blogs/johncassidy/2013/04/the-rogoff-and-reinhart-controversy-a-summing-up.html
163 http://www.voxeu.org/article/debt-and-growth-revisited
164 In the UK, public debt/GDP peaked in 1948 at close to 240%.

Banking crises are often associated with substantial declines in tax revenues and sharp increases in government spending. This is why the indirect costs of banking crises are much larger than the costs of bank bailouts.

As early as March 2009, the IMF warned governments that the global financial system could deteriorate very rapidly once a 'downward credit spiral' gets out of control:

> Policy actions worldwide may not prove to be adequate to deal with the low probability but high impact events that may materialize and undermine global financial stability. Policymakers as a matter of course need to 'think the unthinkable,' and to consider how they would plan to react if contingencies arise.[165]

Mark Carney, the Governor of the Bank of Canada, said at the end of 2011 that our financial system was on the verge of a collapse: 'The global Minsky moment has arrived.'[166]

The Minsky moment, named after American economist Hyman Minsky, is the point in time at which, after decades of prosperity, a wave of selling takes place by parties who had made investments with too much debt. In order to reduce these debts, they even have to sell good investments at increasingly lower prices.

Such a disastrous sell-off of government bonds is one of the major risks we are now facing. At some point, central banks could end up buying almost all their domestic government bonds. Investor money would then flee towards equities and hard assets.

As history has shown (see Appendix I), the general public could start to lose faith in its currency. When enough people lose faith in their country's money, this can lead to hyperinflation.

---

165 http://www.imf.org/external/pubs/ft/survey/so/2008/new031208a.htm
166 http://www.bankofcanada.ca/2011/12/speeches/growth-in-the-age-of-deleveraging/

Once people lose faith in money and its purchasing power, it is almost impossible to re-introduce fiat money.

But according to Jim Rickards hyperinflation could be used by authorities.

> as a policy lever. Hyperinflation produces fairly predictable sets of winners and losers and prompts certain behavior and therefore can be used politically to rearrange social and economic relations among debtors, creditors, labor and capital, while gold is kept available to clean up the wreckage if necessary.

These risks all stem from the unorthodox interventions that central bankers have been implementing since 2008. According to former Fed Chairman Paul Volcker, some of these measures would have been considered unthinkable before the credit crisis.

Chapter 5 – The War on Gold

Deregulation of the financial sector has caused a financial crisis that can only be managed by fraud. Civil damages might be paid, but to halt the fraud itself would mean the collapse of the financial system. Those in charge of the system would prefer the collapse to come from outside, such as from a collapse in the value of the dollar that could be blamed on foreigners, because an outside cause gives them something to blame other than themselves.

– Paul Craig Roberts, Assistant Secretary of the Treasury for Economic Policy under President Reagan (2012)

Why then, is gold the unmentionable four letter word of economics? The answer is threefold; A misunderstanding of the role of money; a misreading of history; and finally, visceral revulsion to the notion that a metal can do a better job of guiding monetary policy than a gaggle of finance ministers, central bankers and well-degreed economists.

– Malcolm Forbes, Forbes Magazine (2002)

Gold has long been viewed by many as a barbarous relic and demonetizing it and phasing it out of the system completely seems to have a good deal of appeal in some quarters.

– Fed-Banker Alfred Hayes, speech for IMF at Economic Club in New York, 31 August 1975

Policymakers are finding it tempting to pursue 'financial repression' - suppressing market prices that they don't like.

– Kevin M. Warsh, former banker of the Fed (2012)

INTRO

The days of the dollar as a world reserve currency are numbered, which explains why gold is making a remarkable comeback and why a flight to hard assets including farm land and old masters has started. Every year, more and more physical gold is moving from vaults in the West to the East as a symbol of a change in the world power balance.

The US wants its dollar system to prevail for as long as possible. It therefore has every vested interest in preventing a 'rush out of dollars towards gold'. By selling (paper) gold, bankers have been trying in the last few decades to keep the price of gold under control. This war on gold has been going on for almost one hundred years,[167] but as I will explain in the following chapters, it gained traction in the 1960s with the forming of the London Gold Pool. Just like the London Gold Pool failed in 1969, the current manipulation scheme of gold (and silver prices) cannot be maintained for much longer. After a decoupling of paper and physical gold prices in the next few years we will see the gold price rise to its 'full potential'.

---

167 It is no coincidence that a book on this topic by the Swiss ex-banker Ferdinand Lips is entitled *Gold Wars*. His book builds upon the research compiled in the pioneering book *War on Gold* by the well-known American researcher Antony Sutton, which came out in 1976.

57. The essence of the war on gold

The war on gold is, in essence, an endeavor to support the dollar. But this is certainly not the only motivation.

According to a number of studies, the level of the gold price and the general public's expectations of inflation are highly correlated. Central bankers work hard to influence inflation expectations. Any Fed/ECB speech is guaranteed to include this expression. A recent Google search on the subject resulted in over 21 million hits.[168] The reasoning behind this can be easily surmised: when people assume that inflation will stay low, they act accordingly and will not be tempted to buy 'hard assets'. A 1988 study by Summers and Barsky confirmed that the price of gold and interest rates are highly correlated as well, with a lower gold price leading to lower interest rates.[169]

The survival of our current financial system depends on people preferring fiat money over gold. After the dollar was taken off the gold standard, bankers have tried to demonetize gold. One of the arguments they use to deter investors from buying gold and silver is that these metals do not deliver a direct return such as interest or dividends. But interest and dividend are payments to compensate for counterparty risk – the risk that your counterparty is unable to live up to its obligations.

168 https://www.google.nl/?gws_rd=cr&ei=4e4zUrOGE4m1owXt3YDIDQ#q='inflation+expectations'
169 Gibson's Paradox and the Gold Standard http://www.gata.org/files/gibson.pdf

58.   Do central banks fear a flight to gold?

If investing in gold undermines our current fiat money system, then central banks have every reason to fear a flight to gold. And apparently they do. I will delve here into examples of the war against gold waged by the Dutch central bank, but similar examples can be found in other countries.

In 2011, a case was brought to court by a small Dutch pension fund, the 'Pensioenfonds Verenigde Glasfabrieken' ('United Glass Factories Pension Fund') against the Dutch central bank (DNB). The pension fund had invested 13% of its assets in physical gold in order to protect its assets from the economic fall-out of the credit crisis, but the DNB had ordered the fund to sell its gold positions. According to documents presented to the court, the DNB was of the opinion that these investments carried too much risk. What makes this statement remarkable is that the DNB has never objected to institutional investors holding too many subprime loans or Greek government bonds in their portfolios. In the end, the DNB lost the court case twice and had to pay compensation to the pension fund.

In another example, investment funds wanting to operate under the international UCITS license are forbidden from being investors in physical gold. This is the only exception made.[170] And Dutch financial entities wanting to take advantage of a special fiscal status known as VBI are allowed to invest in almost any financial asset except physical gold.

The war is being fought not only by central banks but also by commercial financial institutions. Since 2000, most Dutch banks have stopped sales of physical gold to clients. Most of them have also put an end to services enabling clients to store gold in small bank vaults.

---

170 https://www2.blackrock.com/webcore/litService/search/getDocument.
seam?venue=PUB_IND&source=GLOBAL&contentId=1111125006

In 2013, both ABN AMRO and RBS cancelled gold accounts that allowed investors to redeem their value in physical gold. In a letter to clients, ABN AMRO explained that it had changed its precious metals custodian rules and the bank would 'no longer allow physical delivery', only paper settlement.[171]

And US banks are only allowed to advise investors to buy gold shares when they have a gold analyst on their payroll.

As demonstrated, in today's world of finance, it is not that difficult to find numerous examples of central banks and commercial banks working hard to keep investors away from physical gold investments.

171 http://www.zerohedge.com/news/2013-03-24/another-gold-shortage-abn-halt-physical-gold-delivery

59.   Was private ownership of gold ever prohibited?

After the Wall Street crash of 1929, the US economy fell into a deep recession. Four years later, many American banks had collapsed, triggering multiple bank runs. The survival of the financial system was at stake.

To turn the economic tide, President Roosevelt presented an economic recovery plan called 'the New Deal'. The plan included a 'Gold Reserve Act', passed by Congress at the end of January 1934, which empowered the federal government to confiscate all of the Fed's gold and bring it under the US Department of the Treasury. This was a disappointment for most Wall Street bankers who, back in 1913, had taken over not only the monopoly on printing dollars from the Treasury Department but also the entire national gold supply.

At the same time, the dollar was devalued by 69% by raising the exchange rate for gold from $ 20.67 to $ 35 per ounce. With this, the value of the gold that had arrived at the Treasury Department rose by almost $ 3 billion in one day. The dollar's devaluation against gold had an almost immediate effect on the economy. The sale of American products abroad rose, because of the declining value of the dollar. This resulted in increasing industrial production and money supply, while unemployment declined.

Roosevelt also made use of his special presidential authority to issue Executive Order 6102. This prohibited civilians from possessing gold, gold coins or gold certificates. Anyone caught 'hoarding' gold was to be fined $ 10,000 (the equivalent of $ 180,000 today). Several cases of forced gold confiscation were documented. Americans were allowed to keep five ounces of gold at 1933 prices and gold in the form of rare coins. This law remained in force until 1974. Less well known is the fact that all US silver was nationalized at a price of 50 cents per ounce in February 1937.[172]

Another executive order commanded American gold mines to sell their production to the Treasury Department and prohibited the export of gold. In Europe, there has never been a ban on possessing gold. But most countries do have legislation in place allowing governments to ban the possession of gold and/or silver.[173]

172 Business Week, 27 February 1937.
173 Emergency Law on Financial Movement, Article 26 (25 May 1978).

60.   When did the war on gold start?

The first evidence of US meddling in the gold market can be found as early as 1925 when the Fed falsified information regarding the Bank of England's possession of gold in order to influence interest rate levels. [174] However, the war on gold only really took off in the 1960s when trust in the dollar started to fray. Geopolitical conflicts such as the building of the Berlin Wall, the Cuban Missile Crisis and the escalation of violence in Vietnam led to increasing military spending by the US, which in turn resulted in growing US budget deficits. Amid growing concerns in other countries about the value of their dollar reserves as well as signs that they were beginning to accumulate gold, the CIA published a memorandum that presented 'key high-level gold-related deliberations by the then-administration'.[175]

The US strategy is clearly outlined:

- We (the US) lose influence in world affairs whenever:
- – The dollar is weak in exchange markets;
- – There is a major outflow of gold; and/or
- We are obliged to pressure countries into holding dollars.
- To contain these pressures our strategy is:
- – To isolate official from private gold markets by obtaining a pledge from central banks that they will neither buy nor sell gold except to each other;
- – To bring South Africa to sell its current production of gold in the private market, and thus keep the private price down.

An earlier memorandum from 1961 entitled 'US Foreign Exchange Operations: Needs and Methods' described a detailed plan to

---

174 http://www.gata.org/node/8327
175   Read full document here http://www.zerohedge.com/article/cia-chimes-gold-control-highlights-historical-gold-foreign-holdings-shortfunding

manipulate the currency and gold markets via structural interventions in order to support the dollar and maintain the gold price at $ 35 per ounce.[176] It was vital for the US to 'manage' the gold market; otherwise, countries could exchange their surplus dollars for gold and then sell these ounces on the free gold market for a higher price.

176 http://fraser.stlouisfed.org/docs/historical/martin/23_06_19610405.pdf

61. How was the gold price managed?

During meetings of the central bank presidents at the BIS in 1961, it was agreed that a pool of $ 270 million in gold would be made available by the eight participating countries. This so-called 'London Gold Pool'[177] was focused on preventing the gold price from rising above $ 35 per ounce by selling official gold holdings from the central banks gold vaults.

The idea was that if investors attempted to flee to the safe haven of gold, the London Gold Pool would dump gold onto the market in order to keep the gold price from rising. During the Cuban Missile Crisis in 1962, for instance, at least $ 60 million in gold was sold between 22 and 24 October.[178] The IMF provided extra gold to be sold on the market when needed.

Contributions to the London Gold Pool per participating country [179]

US	$ 135 million	(120 tonnes)
Germany	$ 30 million	(27 tonnes)
England	$ 25 million	(22 tonnes)
Italy	$ 25 million	(22 tonnes)
France	$ 25 million	(22 tonnes)
Switzerland	$ 10 million	(9 tonnes)
The Netherlands	$ 10 million	(9 tonnes)
Belgium	$ 10 million	(9 tonnes)
Total	$ 270 million	

The participating countries also had to declare that they would not buy gold in the open market from countries such as Russia

177 Ferdinand Lips, *Gold Wars* (2002).

178 Ferdinand Lips, *Gold Wars* (2002).

179 The UK lost 1800 tonnes between 1960 and 1971 and its gold holdings decreased from almost 2500 tonnes in 1960 to just over 310 metric tonnes at the end of 2013

or South Africa. In true BIS fashion, these agreements were not put on paper, thereby ensuring complete secrecy.[180].

In 2010, a number of previously secret US telex reports from 1968 were made public by Wikileaks.[181] These messages describe what had to be done in order to keep the gold price under control. The aim was to convince investors that it was completely pointless to speculate on a rise in the price of gold. One of the reports mentions a propaganda campaign to convince the public that the central banks would remain 'the masters of gold'. Despite these efforts, in March 1968, the London Gold Pool was disbanded because France would no longer cooperate. The London gold market remained closed for two weeks. In other gold markets around the world, gold immediately rose 25% in value.

France even stepped out of the command structure of the NATO.[182] This was a remarkable step considering the danger that the Soviet Union posed to the European continent during the Cold War. It clearly shows France was distancing itself more and more from the US.

The end of the London Gold Pool was the starting shot of a 'bull market' in gold which would last for 13 years and which would see the gold price increasing by over 2,500%.

180 This agreement was disclosed by Charles A. Coombs, who was responsible for gold transactions at that time, in his strikingly open biography, (1960).
181 http://www.zerohedge.com/article/declassified-state-dept-data-highlights-global-high-level-arrangement-remain-masters-gold
182 http://www.dailymail.co.uk/news/article-1161642/As-France-rejoins-NATO-humorous-reminder-missed-them.html

62.   The IMF's role in the war on gold

In response to the 'gold shortage' during the years of the London Gold Pool, in 1963 the IMF created a new form of international reserve assets called special drawing rights (SDR). These were created out of thin air and were designed to take over the dollar's role as a world reserve currency when needed.[183] Because SDRs were created out of nothing, they soon received the nickname 'paper gold'.

Since 1975, the Americans have worked with the IMF time and again to try to control the gold market by unloading tons of gold. Below are some examples of IMF gold transactions, made during times of stress in physical gold markets.[184] (All quotes are from the IMF website):

1970–1971
To support the dollar: 'The IMF sold gold to member countries in amounts roughly corresponding to those purchased from South Africa during this period.'

1956–1972
To save the dollar: 'In order to generate income to offset operational deficits, some IMF gold was sold to the United States and the proceeds invested in US government securities.'

---

183 The IMF initially defined the SDR in terms of a fixed amount of gold, then equal to one dollar, and allocated 9.3 billion SDRs between 1970 and 1972 in proportion to member countries' quotas in the IMF. The IMF redefined the SDR as a weighted average of the US dollar, the British pound, the Japanese yen, and the currencies that eventually comprised the euro and made a second allocation of 21.4 billion SDRs between 1979 and 1981. Nevertheless, the SDR quickly devolved for the most part into a unit of account that was primarily used on the IMF's books. SDRs can be converted into whatever currency a borrower requires at exchange rates based on a weighted basket of international currencies. The IMF has typically lent to countries using funds denominated in SDRs.

184 http://www.imf.org/external/np/exr/facts/gold.htm

1976–1980

To dampen explosion of gold price: 'The IMF sold approximately one-third, 50 million ounces, of its then-existing gold holdings following an agreement by its member countries to reduce the role of gold in the international monetary system.'

1999–2000

To meet substantial Y2K-demand: 'In December 1999, the Executive Board authorized off-market transactions in gold of up to 14 million ounces.'

2009

To meet huge post-Lehman demand and when gold broke the $ 1,000 level: 'On September 18, 2009, the Executive Board approved the sale of 400 tons of gold which amounted to one-eighth of the Fund's total holdings of gold at that time.'[185]

A 1999 press release from the IMF communications department 'spinned' the gold sales with the text; 'to help finance the IMF's participation in the Heavily Indebted Poor Countries (HIPC) Initiative'.

When the IMF sold another 200 tonnes of gold in 2012,[186] it communicated that at least 90% of the profits would be made available for the Poverty Reduction and Growth Trust (PRGT).[187]

185 http://www.imf.org/external/np/sec/pr/2009/pr09310.htm
186 http://www.imf.org/external/np/sec/pr/2012/pr1256.htm
187 http://www.imf.org/external/np/exr/facts/gold.htm

63.   How did the IMF amass its gold reserves?

The IMF received most of its gold from member countries, which had to pay 25% of their funding quotas to the IMF in physical bullion. This was because gold played a central role in the international monetary system until the collapse of the Bretton Woods agreements in 1971. Seven years later, the IMF fundamentally changed the role of gold in the international monetary system by eliminating its use as the common denominator of the post-World War II exchange rate system and ended its obligatory use in transactions between the IMF and its member countries.

For years, gold analysts have wondered whether a form of double counting of national and IMF gold reserves had occurred. In a reaction, the IMF stated in 2009: 'Members do not include IMF gold within their own reserves because it is an asset of the IMF. Members include their reserve position in the fund in their international reserves.'[188] This means that the value of IMF gold positions can be found on the balance sheets of both the IMF and member countries.

An analyst who studied this subject extensively published his findings on his blog:[189]

> Between 1958 and 1959 there was a first major increase in IMF gold since 1945. This boosted institutional gold holdings by 797 tons. At the same time, central bank holdings – the supposed source of this gold – fell by just 48 tons... the IMF owns the gold and doesn't lend it (out), but because it's held under earmark for members, the members themselves can lend it (and include it in their own stated gold reserves).

188 http://arch09.goldtent.net/2009/04/03/find-the-imf-goldstolen-from-nearby-castle-sorry/
189 http://theostrichhead.typepad.com/index/2010/04/imf-gold-holdings-why-mine-the-stuff-when-your-accountants-can-create-it.html

Another acknowledgement of the double counting can be found in an IMF paper from 2006.[190]

> RESTEG[191] agreed that double counting issues may arise for both allocated and unallocated gold from outright sales of gold acquired through gold swaps/loans. Some suggested that a solution to this double counting needs to be considered, although some noted that such double counting is not a new issue.[192]

Centralbanking.com, a website specialized in central banking news, published a story on this subject under the title 'IMF admits double counting gold'.[193]

---

190 http://www.imf.org/external/np/sta/bop/pdf/resteg11.pdf

191 RESTEG stands for reserve assets technical expert group, the IMF committee on balance of payment statistics.

192 As a consequence, experts on double counting estimate that half of the 30,000 tonnes of official total gold reserves could in fact have already been lent out and sold by national central banks.

193 http://www.centralbanking.com/central-banking/news/1407346/imf-admits-double-counting-gold

64. Are there more cases of double counting in the US?

In the US national gold reserves can be found on two different balance sheets.[194] When Wall Street bankers founded the Fed in 1913, they not only took over the monopoly to print dollars from the government, they also 'confiscated' the national gold reserves, which ended up on the Fed's balance sheet. President Roosevelt nationalized gold in 1933, and transferred the Fed's gold reserves back to the US Treasury Department. However, the Treasury issued gold certificates to the Reserve Banks,[195] therefore this gold also still appears on the Federal Reserve balance sheet.[196]

Former Republican senator Ron Paul inquired in 2011 whether these 'gold vouchers' issued to the Federal Reserve banks give them the authority to demand and receive gold from the Treasury Department. The General Counsel of the Fed, Scott Alvarez, summoned by the US Congress, would only confirm that the 'gold certificates' were accounting documents and were part of the banks' balance sheets.[197]

More examples can be found in the world of paper gold and gold trackers. Exchange Traded Funds, or ETFs, have become significant players in the gold and silver markets. An ETF follows an underlying index or value as accurately as possible. These funds have become popular because they are tradeable just like shares but at much lower costs. Since 1993, more than 700 ETFs have been introduced which follow all sorts of indices and commodities.[198]

---

194 http://www.federalreserve.gov/releases/h41/current/
195 http://www.coinweek.com/bullion-report/fed-releases-document-proving-it-has-lied-about-gold-swaps-and-gold-price-manipulation/
196 If there were to be a revaluation of gold, the certificates would also be revalued upwards.
197 http://www.globalresearch.ca/us-gold-reserve-audit-show/5326810
198 http://www.nyse.com/pdfs/ETFS7109.pdf

Gold ETFs are supposed to be fully backed by gold bars, as stated in their prospectus. A gold ETF therefore follows the price of gold with physical gold as security. However, there are many who doubt whether ETFs actually possess physical gold. As reported by Forbes magazine in 2011:

> Skeptics have raised doubts over the trust's management of its physical gold, with questions over how much is actually held. HSBC, the custodian, is very secretive regarding its vault. Earlier this year, CNBC's Bob Pisani was allowed to see the vault only after surrendering his cell phone and taken in a van with blacked out windows to an undisclosed location. Once in the vault, Pisani held up a gold bar and explained they were all numbered and registered. Astutely, Zerohedge noted the bar Pisani held up was missing from the current bar list, fueling further speculation and skepticism.

Another analyst discovered that the serial number of the same 'unique' gold bar held up by Pisani could be found on a list of another gold ETF.

65. How often have US gold reserves in Fort Knox been audited?

In 1933, after President Roosevelt forced Americans to sell their gold to the US Treasury, a larger storage space was needed for the government's gold reserves. New vaults were constructed for this purpose in Fort Knox, Kentucky. The Fort Knox vaults now house some 4,500 metric tons of gold bullion, roughly 3% of all the gold ever refined. This the second largest depository in the United States. The largest is in Manhattan and is the underground vault of the Federal Reserve Bank of New York, which holds some 7,000 metric tons, some in trust for foreign nations.

A few random audits of the gold in Fort Knox were carried out between 1974 and 1986,[199] but doubts about the US gold reserves have continued to grow. Former Congressman Ron Paul, who was a Republican presidential candidate in 2012 and chairman of the US House Financial Services Subcommittee on Domestic Monetary Policy, has questioned the US Treasury about the gold reserves for years. He even called for an audit of the gold reserves in 2011, but his request was denied.[200] The Treasury Department did release the results of an audit on the Treasury's gold holdings stored at the New York Fed in 2010, but the official gold reserves in Fort Knox have never been audited.[201]

In 1981, a number of newspaper reports surfaced about missing Fort Knox gold. An article by the British *Sunday Express* entitled 'United States Probes Fort Knox Robbery' focuses on some 165.1 million ounces of gold which the United States allegedly lost between 1961 and 1971. The newspaper quotes Dr. Peter Beter, a financial adviser to the late President John Kennedy, who be-

---

199 http://www.globalresearch.ca/us-gold-reserve-audit-show/5326810
200 http://money.cnn.com/2011/06/24/news/economy/ron_paul_gold_audit/
201 For security reasons, no visitors are allowed inside the depository grounds. The only exception was an inspection by members of the US Congress and the news media on 23 September 1974.

lieves the theft occurred in the late 1960s when the United States transferred 233 million ounces from Fort Knox to the Federal Reserve Bank in New York and London's Bank of England. According to the article, 23.1 million ounces were accounted for at the Federal Reserve Bank while another 45.2 million ounces arrived safely in England. The destination of the remaining 165.1 million ounces is unknown, and Dr. Beter stated that attempts to learn what happened have been 'stonewalled' by Treasury officials.

The official reaction from Jerry Nisenson, Deputy Director of Gold Market Activities at the Treasury Department, was strange to say the least: 'We have investigated the claims of Dr. Beter and his supporters and we contend that the gold was not stolen. There is no cover-up. They have misinterpreted our books. The gold was being refined into better quality gold and those ounces just went up the chimney.' The possibility of irregularities at the US Assay Office in New York, through which all the gold was shipped, was also noted in an item in Money Magazine in January 1980.

The discovery of some gold-plated tungsten[202] bars only increased rumours about gold bars being changed into 'fake gold bars'.

As the US government refuses to allow an audit of Fort Knox, even after repeated requests from one of its senators, these kinds of rumours are bound to continue circulating.[203]

202 Tungsten has nearly the same weight as gold.
203 http://fofoa.blogspot.nl/2009/11/is-dollar-good-as-tungsten.htm

66.   Did the game plan change after 1980?

In his book *Deception and Abuse at the Fed*, Robert D. Auerbach explains how the Fed even misleads Congress about its monetary policies. While the Fed is obliged by law to record its FOMC meetings, it had claimed for years that no transcripts exist. Eventually the truth came out that Chairman Alan Greenspan had instructed all tapes and accounts to be destroyed. Only transcripts since the end of the 1970s have been archived.

From the transcript of a March 1978 meeting, we know that the manipulation of the gold price was a point of discussion.[204] During the meeting, then Fed Chairman Miller pointed out that it was not even necessary to sell gold in order to bring the price down. According to him, it was enough to bring out a statement that the Fed was intending to sell gold.

This form of 'expectation management' has since become more the rule than the exception. Time and again, it has been communicated through press communiqués that the Fed or the IMF was considering selling gold, and time and again we have seen the gold price fall as a result.

Even as faith in the dollar was restored during the 1980s, the Fed understood that it had to continue fighting gold. In March 1993, the Federal Reserve board discussed how inflation expectations are influenced by the price of gold. When people doubt the value of fiat money, they tend to seek refuge in gold, which drives the price up. This scenario has since become reality following the fall of Lehman Brothers. Chairman Alan Greenspan suggested the US Treasury could sell a small portion of US gold reserves. The transcript runs as follows:

Board member Angel: The price of gold is largely determined by what people who do not have trust in fiat money system

204 http://www.federalreserve.gov/monetarypolicy/files/FOMC19930518meeting.pdf

want to use for an escape out of any currency, and they want to gain security through owning gold...

Greenspan: I have one other issue I'd like to throw on the table. I hesitate to do it, but let me tell you some of the issues that are involved here. If we are dealing with psychology, then the thermometers one uses to measure it have an effect. I was raising the question on the side with Governor Mullins of what would happen if the Treasury sold a little gold in this market. There's an interesting question here because if the gold price broke in that context, the thermometer would not be just a measuring tool. It would basically affect the underlying psychology.

Greenspan explained that a drop in the gold price would lower inflation expectations. He wanted to change the dynamics of the gold price so that it would no longer be an alarm bell for inflation.

Because the US Treasury is not legally allowed to sell its gold reserves, the Fed decided in 1995 to examine whether it was possible to set up a special construction whereby so-called 'gold swaps' could bring in gold from the gold reserves of Western central banks.

In this construction, the gold would be 'swapped' with the Fed, which would then be sold by Wall Street banks in order to keep prices down. Because of the 'swap agreement', the gold is officially only lent out, so Western central banks could keep it on their balance sheets as 'gold receivables'.

It was a wonderful plan. The Fed started informing foreign central bankers that they expected the gold price to decline further, and large quantities of central banks' gold became available to sell in the open market. Logistically this was an easy operation, since the New York Fed vaults had the largest collection of foreign gold holdings. Since the 1930s, many Western countries had chosen to store their gold safely in the US out of fears of a German or Soviet invasion.

A number of European banks were ready to provide gold to help the Fed. In a Congress hearing in 1998, Greenspan remarked: 'Central banks stand ready to lend out enough gold if the gold price rises.'[205]

Vast amounts of gold were sold in this way at the end of the 1990s. An estimated 1,000 tonnes of physical gold were dumped each year. Since yearly worldwide gold mine production at the time was just over 2,000 tonnes, the gold price kept on dropping until it almost touched a 20-year bottom of $ 250 an ounce in 1999.

The annual reports of many central banks show the results of these gold swaps. Reports published by the Dutch central (DNB) reveal an entry labeled 'gold and gold receivables', whereas in the 1980s, only 'gold' is mentioned as an entry.

Central bank gold reserves _____

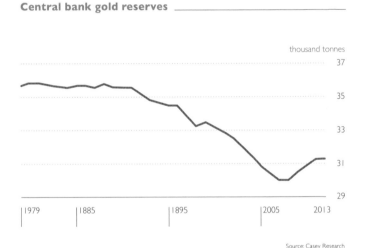

Source: Casey Research

205 United States of America Congressional Records.

67. Didn't the British help by unloading gold in 1999?

Between 1999 and 2002, the UK embarked on an aggressive selling of its gold reserves, when gold prices were at their lowest in 20 years. Prior to starting, the Chancellor of the Exchequer, Gordon Brown, announced that the UK would be selling more than half of its gold reserves in a series of auctions in order to diversify the assets of the UK's reserves.

The markets' reaction was one of shock, because sales of gold reserves by governments had until then always taken place without any advance warning to investors. Brown was following the Fed's strategy of inducing a fall in the gold price via an announcement of possible sales. Brown's move was therefore not intended to receive the best price for its gold but rather to bring down the price of gold as low as possible. The advance notice of the sales drove the price of gold down by 10% just before the first auction on 6 July 1999. The UK eventually sold almost 400 tons of gold over 17 auctions in just three years, just as the gold market was bottoming out.

There has always been much speculation about the real reason for the British gold dumping, which greatly helped the US. As I explained earlier, a lower gold price supports the dollar as a world reserve currency. Demand for physical gold was relatively high in 1999 due to the signing of the Washington Agreement on Gold in September 1999. This agreement was made after several gold-producing (African) countries had protested against the ongoing dumping of gold during the 1990s. In the five-year agreement (1999-2004), European central banks agreed to limit their total gold sales to 400 tonnes per year.

This announcement triggered a sharp rise in the price of gold, from $ 260 to $ 330 per ounce within two weeks. Another reason for the high demand was fears concerning the Millennium Bug[206] which was associated with the rollover of the millennium (Y2K). To meet the significant Y2K-related demand, the IMF[207] also sold 14 million ounces in December 1999 (as mentioned earlier).

Gordon Brown's sale of the UK's gold reserves probably came about following a request from the US.[208] In 1999, some US banks that had gone 'short' gold, became mired in trouble when the gold prices moved up sharply that year. The situation was so bad that a bank collapse seemed imminent. The Telegraph reported in 2012:

> One globally significant US bank in particular is understood to have been heavily short on two tonnes of gold, enough to call into question its solvency if redemption occurred at the prevailing price. Goldman Sachs, which is not understood to have been significantly short on gold itself, is rumoured to have approached the Treasury to explain the situation through its then head of commodities Gavyn Davies, later chairman of the BBC and married to Sue Nye who ran Brown's private office.[209]

According to The Telegraph, the Chancellor then took the decision to bail them out by dumping Britain's gold. This forced down the price of gold and allowed the banks to buy back gold even at a profit, thus meeting their borrowing obligations.

---

206 In the late 1990s, reports appeared in the press about a possible collapse of complex banking networks because computer systems mostly use only two digits instead of four for date programming. Many feared that systems would run aground because computer clocks would switch to 1900 instead of 2000.

207 http://www.imf.org/external/np/exr/facts/gold.htm

208 The US has since fully supported Mr. Brown's political career, particularly in his bid to become prime minister in 2007. Media reports from 2010 indicate that the decision to sell was made by Brown (Treasury) and was not welcomed by the Bank of England. (Zerohedge)

209 The telegraph, november 27th, 2012.

According to Zerohedge,[210] the Governor of the Bank of England Eddie George told the following story to several people in a private conversation in September 1999:

We looked into the abyss if the gold price rose further. A further rise would have taken down one or several trading houses, which might have taken down all the rest in their wake. At any cost we had to quell the gold price. It was very difficult to get gold under control but we have now succeeded. The US Fed was very active in getting the gold price down. So was the UK.

210 http://www.zerohedge.com/article/did-gordon-brown-sell-uks-gold-keep-aig-and-rothschild-solvent-more-disclosures-how-ny-fed-m

68. Further evidence of systematic gold price suppression

The central bank of Australia confirmed in 2003 that its gold reserves are mainly used to control the price of gold. In its 2003 annual report, the Reserve Bank of Australia stated: 'Foreign currency reserve assets and gold are held primarily to support intervention in the foreign exchange market'.[211]

A top official of the BIS, William R. White, confirmed this line of thinking at a conference in 2005. In his opinion, there are five important tasks for central banks, one of which is to influence gold prices and other currencies. He described this as 'the provision of international credits and joint efforts to influence asset prices (especially gold and foreign exchange) in circumstances where this might be thought useful.'[212]

Central banks have even used at least one gold mining company to help them keep the price of gold under control. This became apparent in a lawsuit started in 2003 by gold dealer Blanchard against producer Barrick Gold Corporation and JPMorganChase. Barrick confirmed it had borrowed gold from Western central banks through 'swap agreements' at the request of the Federal Reserve in order to sell this gold on the market.[213] Coincidentally, former President George Bush Senior was working as an advisor to Barrick in the period that these remarkable trades occurred.[214] In its defense, Barrick claimed that it was acting on orders from the Federal Reserve, positioning itself as a sort of agent acting on behalf of central banks.

211 http://www.rba.gov.au/publications/annual-reports/rba/2003/pdf/2003-report.pdf
212 William R. White, Basel 2005.
213 http://www.gata.org/files/BarrickConfessionMotionToDismiss.pdf
214 http://www.gata.org/files/BarrickConfessionMotionToDismiss.pdf

69.   Recent methods to manipulate the gold price

The transition from open outcry (where traders stand in a trading pit and shout out orders) to electronic trading gave new opportunities for Wall Street (and the Fed) to control financial markets. Wall Street veteran lawyer Jim Rickards presented a paper in 2006 in which he explained how 'derivatives could be used to manipulate underlying physical markets such as oil, copper and gold'.[215] In his bestseller entitled *Currency Wars*, he explains how the prohibition of derivatives regulation in the Commodity Futures Modernization Act (2000) had 'opened the door to exponentially greater size and variety in these instruments that are now hidden off the balance sheets of the major banks, making them almost impossible to monitor'.

These changes made it much easier to manipulate financial markets, especially because prices for metals such as gold and silver are set by trading future contracts on the global markets. Because up to 99% of these transactions are conducted on behalf of speculators who do not aim for physical delivery and are content with paper profits, markets can be manipulated by selling large amounts of contracts in gold, silver or other commodities (on paper).

Especially since the start of the credit crisis, market participants have now and again been bombarding precious metal futures markets with a tsunami of sell orders. The price of gold was forced down by $ 200 during a two-day raid[216] in April 2013, and silver was sent 35% lower in three days in September 2011.

Another example was the decline in the silver price on 1 May 2011. On the previous Friday, the silver price had reached a record level of just over $ 50 an ounce. In technical terms, a double top was formed (in 1980 the silver price reached $ 50 as well). This

---

215 Jim Rickards, *Currency Wars* (2011)
216 According to a study by analyst Grant Williams, the chance of a two-day attack (a standard deviation move of that size on both days) is one in a billion.

made silver vulnerable to an attack by technical traders. The raid started soon after midnight when futures trading in the digital gold and silver market began. Both the Japanese and UK financial markets were closed due to holidays. The normally meager market was now therefore extremely thin. Appearing as if out of 'thin' air, the market was soon swamped with (digital) selling orders.

In a study analyzing all intraday gold price changes between 2002 and 2012, the German analyst Dimitri Speck found that average gold prices fell consistently and significantly during New York trading hours.[217]

In 2011, the Deutsche Bank sent a proposal to its high-profile clients on how to profit from the 'suppression of the gold price'. This is another indication that insiders are well aware of these malversations and even manage to profit from it.

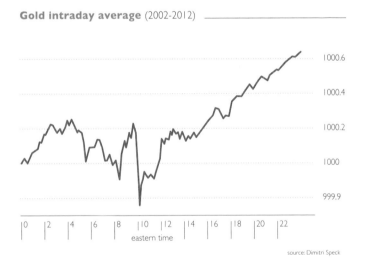

Gold intraday average (2002-2012)

source: Dimitri Speck

217 http://www.seasonal-charts.com/intraday_metalle_gold.html

70.   More evidence of manipulation of precious metal markets

During a hearing by the US Commodity Futures Trading Commission (CFTC) at the end of 2009, professional silver trader Andrew Maguire came forward to recount how he had witnessed planned attacks on the price of silver. Maguire informed the commission he had overheard how traders used to boast how much money they made by manipulating gold and silver markets. In an email to CFTC commissioners Chilton and Ramirez, Maguire explains how Wall Street traders manipulated the precious metals markets especially around days with option expiries and important economic news announcements.

> From: Andrew Maguire
> Sent: Tuesday, January 26, 2010 12:51 PM
> To: Ramirez, Eliud [CFTC]
> Cc: Chilton, Bart [CFTC]
> Subject: Silver today
>
> Dear Mr. Ramirez:
>
> I thought you might be interested in looking into the silver trading today. It was a good example of how a single seller, when they hold such a concentrated position in the very small silver market, can instigate a selloff at will. These events trade to a regular pattern and we see orchestrated selling occur 100% of the time at options expiry, contract rollover, non-farm payrolls[218] (no matter if the news is bullish or bearish), and in a lesser way at the daily silver fix.

218 Non-farm payrolls refers to the statistic provided each month by the US Bureau of Labor showing the change in employment excluding government and farm employees.

The CFTC commissioner Ramirez replied a day later:

> From: Ramirez, Eliud [CFTC]
> To: Andrew Maguire
> Sent: Wednesday, January 27, 2010 4:04 PM
> Subject: RE: Silver today
>
> Mr. Maguire,
>
> Thank you for this communication, and for taking the time
> to furnish the slides.

In January 2010, Maguire had even warned the CFTC about a
coming attack, describing in detail how gold and silver prices
would be hit the moment the non-farm payrolls number was
made public. The hit occurred exactly as Maguire had predicted:

> From: Andrew Maguire
> To: Ramirez, Eliud [CFTC]
> Cc: BChilton [CFTC]
> Sent: Wednesday, February 03, 2010 3:18 PM
>
> Thought it may be helpful to your investigation if I gave you
> the heads up for a manipulative event signaled for Friday,
> 5th Feb. The non-farm payrolls number will be announced
> at 8.30 ET. There will be one of two scenarios occurring,
> and both will result in silver (and gold) being taken down
> with a wave of short selling designed to take out obvious
> support levels and trip stops below. While I will no doubt be
> able to profit from this upcoming trade, it is an example of
> just how easy it is to manipulate a market if a concentrated
> position is allowed by a very small group of traders.
> I am aware that physical buyers in large size are awaiting
> this event to scoop up as much 'discounted' gold and silver
> as possible. These are sophisticated entities, mainly foreign,

who know how to play the short sellers and turn this paper gold into real delivered physical.

And another email by Maguire after the attack occurred:

From: Andrew Maguire
To: Ramirez, Eliud [CFTC]
Cc: BChilton [CFTC]; GGensler [CFTC]
Sent: Friday, February 05, 2010 3:37 PM
Subject: Fw: Silver today.

A final e-mail to confirm that the silver manipulation was a great success and played out EXACTLY to plan as predicted yesterday. How would this be possible if the silver market was not in the full control of the parties we discussed in our phone interview? I have honored my commitment not to publicize our discussions.
I hope you took note of how and who added the short sales (I certainly have a copy) and I am certain you will find it is the same concentrated shorts who have been in full control since JPM took over the Bear Stearns position.

71. Investigations into manipulation in precious metals markets

Silver analyst Ted Butler has asked the US CFTC repeatedly over a period of 27 years to look into the possible manipulation of silver markets.[219] According to Butler, the CFTC 'has conducted three formal reviews into whether silver was manipulated in the last nine years alone'. In the first two, the agency concluded that no manipulation existed. Until 2008, the CFTC had on several occasions denied that manipulation in silver was taking place.[220]

Continuous complaints and several petitions by silver investors worldwide resulted in a third investigation into the silver market. In September 2008, the CFTC confirmed that its Division of Enforcement has been investigating 'complaints of misconduct in the silver market'.[221, 222] The investigation went on for more than five years. Although Butler was directly involved in bringing about all three reviews, he has never heard anything back from the CFTC and was never interviewed.

CFTC commissioner Bart Chilton has said on different occasions that he believed there had been 'fraudulent efforts' to 'deviously control' the silver price.[223] He also made some public comments about the large concentration on the short side of COMEX silver. These comments resulted in a civil class action lawsuit being filed against JPMorgan, who holds a majority of these positions.[224]

---

219 http://www.cftc.gov/index.htm 'Ensuring the integrity of the futures & options markets'
220 http://www.bloomberg.com/news/2010-10-26/silver-market-faced-fraudulent-efforts-to-control-price-chilton-says.html
221 http://wsf.typepad.com/wall-street-forecaster/2011/11/cftc-statement-regarding-enforcement-investigation-of-the-silver-markets.html
222 http://www.cftc.gov/PressRoom/PressReleases/silvermarketstatement
223 http://www.scribd.com/doc/65207178/11-09-12-FINAL-Consolidated-Class-Action-Complaint
224 http://seekingalpha.com/article/234051-cftc-investigates-jpmorgan-hsbc-silver-market-manipulation-may-have-kept-prices-down

A New York judge dismissed the lawsuit at the end of December 2012.

In March 2013, reports surfaced about another CFTC investigation into whether prices were being manipulated in the world's largest gold market.[225] The CFTC inquiry apparently now also involved the gold markets.

But after its five-year investigation into complaints of misconduct regarding silver prices, in 2013 the CFTC concluded there was no ground for claims of manipulation of the silver markets.

In september 2010, Zerohedge reported one of the two administrative judges for the CFTC has written and filed a 'Notice and Order' saying:

> There are two administrative law judges at the Commodity Futures Trading Commission: myself and the Honorable Bruce Levine. On Judge Levine's first week on the job, nearly twenty years ago, he came into my office and stated that he had promised Wendy Gramm, then Chairwoman of the Commission, that we would never rule in a Complainant's favor. A review of his rulings will confirm that he has fulfilled his vow. Jedge Levine, in the cynical guise of enforcing the rules, forces pro se complaints to run a hostile procedural gauntlet until they lose hope, and either withdraw their complaint or settle for a pittance, regardless of the merits of the case.

225 http://online.wsj.com/article/SB10001424127887324077704578358381575462340.html#printMode

72.   Do regulators now want Wall Street to stop trading commodities?

The Federal Reserve announced in the summer of 2013 that 'it might reconsider its decade-old policy which has allowed investment banks to diversify and own certain unrelated businesses such as participation in the physical commodity markets'.[226] CFTC commissioner Bart Chilton remarked in the same week: 'I don't want banks owning warehouses, whether they have aluminum, gold, silver, or anything else in them.' These statements indicate the start of coordinated action by the Fed and the CFTC towards Wall Street banks active in commodities.

Around the same time, a letter from the CFTC to the Federal Reserve was leaked to the public by CNBC.[227] In the letter, the CFTC is 'urging the Fed to firmly draft the final Volcker Rule in a way that ensures banks can no longer speculate in commodity markets'. And Bloomberg reported on the same day that the CFTC had even sent letters to banks asking them 'not to destroy documents relating to warehouses registered by exchanges such as the London Metal Exchange (LME) or Chicago Mercantile Exchange (COMEX)'. We have increasing evidence, therefore, that regulators are starting to make a move in this area.

That same year, JPMorgan made a surprising announcement[228] that it had sold its office building at One Chase Manhattan Plaza to China's largest industrial group.[229] To precious metal watchers, this address is best known for its enormous precious metal vaults. The vaults are situated 80 feet below ground level at 33 Liberty Street. It used to contain up to 20% of the world's gold. Strangely

226 http://www.bloomberg.com/news/2013-08-05/fed-should-reverse-commodity-trading-policy-cftc-s-chilton-says.html
227 http://www.cnbc.com/id/100937811/print
228 http://www.huffingtonpost.com/nathan-lewis/wheres-the-gold_b_216896.html
229 http://www.bloomberg.com/news/2013-10-18/jpmorgan-selling-chase-manhattan-plaza-in-nyc-to-china-s-fosun.html

enough, the sale was realized shortly after reports surfaced[230] that almost all of JPMorgan's gold holdings had been withdrawn from its warehouse at Chase Manhattan Plaza.

Zerohedge discovered earlier that the JPMorgan vaults were situated right across from the Fed's own gold vault:

> ...we have learned that the world's largest private, and commercial, gold vault, that belonging once upon a time to Chase Manhattan, and now to JPMorgan Chase, is located, right across the street, and at the same level underground, resting just on top of the Manhattan bedrock, as the vault belonging to the New York Federal Reserve, which according to folklore is the official location of the biggest collection of sovereign, public gold in the world.

But the most stunning revelation was the fact that 'the Chase Plaza is linked to the (Fed) facility via tunnels'.[231]

The news[232] of JPMorgan's sale of its Chase Manhattan Plaza office came only weeks after the bank announced that it was 'pursuing strategic alternatives for its physical commodities business, including its holdings of commodities assets' and that 'it plans to get out of the business of owning and trading physical commodities ranging from metals to oil'. Both developments appear to be related. The fact that the Chinese company was allowed to buy the largest private gold vaults just across from the Fed's gold vaults in the heart of the financial district of Manhattan, is an indication that an agreement may have been made between China and the US about the storage of China's gold.

230 http://sufiy.blogspot.co.uk/2013/07/jpm-gold-vault-chronicles-eligible-gold.html
231 http://www.zerohedge.com/news/2013-03-02/why-jpmorgans-gold-vault-largest-world-located-next-new-york-fed
232 http://www.zerohedge.com/news/2013-07-26/jpmorgan-exit-physical-commodity-business

73. Why has this gold manipulation not been reported on before?

This has all been reported before,[233] but the mainstream financial media have so far neglected to pick up this story. Since 2004, a considerable number of studies about the manipulation of gold and/or silver markets have been published.

1 – The famous Canadian investor Eric Sprott published an extensive study in 2004 called *Not Free, Not Fair – the Long-Term Manipulation of the Gold Price*[234] in which he discusses the manipulation of the gold price.

2 – In 2006, the London broker Cheuvreux, a part of Credit Agricole, published a report[235] in connection with 'the management' of the gold price under the title *Remonetization of Gold: Start Hoarding*. The authors concluded that by lending out gold, Western central banks possessed only half of the recorded 30,000 tonnes of global official gold reserves.

3 – A year later, Citigroup analysts John H. Hill and Graham Wark brought out their own report *Gold: Riding the Reflationary Rescue* in which they explain that gold 'undoubtedly faced headwinds this year from resurgent central bank selling, which was clearly timed to cap the gold price'. This selling, according to Citigroup, was clearly intended to prevent a further rise in the price of gold.[236]

These studies also disclose information about a a class-action lawsuit brought against Morgan Stanley in 2007,[237] for charging storage fees for precious metals, but the clients argued that the Wall Street bank neither bought nor stored the metals.

233 http://www.mineweb.com/mineweb/content/en/mineweb-political-economy?oid=101525&sn=Detail
234 http://www.sprott.com/media/105296/not-free-not-fair.pdf
235 http://www.gata.org/files/CheuvreuxGoldReport.pdf
236 http://www.gata.org/node/5568/
237 http://uk.reuters.com/article/2007/06/12/morganstanley-suit-idUKN1228014520070612

Chapter 6 – The Big Reset

Gold is money, everything else is credit.
  – J.P. Morgan (1906)

I hate to see gold rise because then I know all else is falling apart.
  – Larry Kudlow, CNBC (2006)

The global financial system, that has produced more and more credit in increasingly easier ways, possibly has reached the point that it can no longer operate in an official way.
  – Bill Gross, founder of investment company PIMCO (2012)

Rising prices of precious metals and other commodities are an indication of a very early stage of an endeavour to move away from paper currencies.
  – Alan Greenspan, former Chairman of the Fed (2009)

Any overt Chinese declaration on the central role of gold would automatically damp Chinese people's faith in fiat currencies and could promote an unhealthy over-interest in the metal, with negative effects on the country's stability... China may announce a rise in gold reserves, as a result of accumulation over a reasonably long period, at a time that makes sense for the Chinese authorities. This points to a possible announcement at some time in the future when the gold price may be unambiguously rising.
  – Official Monetary and Financial Institutions Forum (OMFIF), *Gold, the renminbi and the multi-currency reserve system* (2012)

INTRO

The world economy and its currency system can be compared to supertankers. All route changes have to be planned well in advance. If history has taught us anything, it is that a currency tends to lose its world reserve status over a long period of transition. The 'endgame' is often drawn out over decennia. The British pound first suspended its gold standard[238] at the start of World War I in 1914, but it was not until 1944 before the dollar became its successor (during the last Big Reset).

Although the US understands that the dollar will one day lose its world reserve currency status, the Americans will try to maintain their monetary supremacy for as long as possible. Actually, it was already apparent to the Americans back in 1971 that the endgame for this dollar-based system had begun.[239] For over 40 years, the US has used all its power, creativity and flexibility to keep its monetary allies on board. Every trick in the book has been used to convince countries to support the dollar and to marginalize the role of gold.

But since the Fed has started to monetize most of the newly issued debt as part of its QE operations, the point of no return has been passed. Probably even before 2020, the global financial system will have to find a different anchor. There are only two options: a reset planned well in advance or one that is implemented following a monetary crisis. We can expect the US to take the initiative again before a real crisis of confidence occurs.

238 In an attempt to reintroduce stability, a variation on the gold standard was reintroduced in 1925. This was abandoned on 21 September 1931.
239 Note that Nixon himself said in his TV adress that day: 'we will press for the necessary reforms for an urgently needed new international monetary system'.

74. Why do you expect a Big Reset of the global financial system?

Our financial system can be changed in almost any way as long as the main world trading partners can agree to the changes. There are two types of resets: those that are planned well in advance – such as the Bretton Woods reset in 1944 which affected almost the whole world – and smaller resets needed due to monetary developments. Examples of the latter are the introduction of the gold-backed D-Mark after the Weimar hyperinflation in 1923 in Germany, the closing of the gold window by the US in 1971, and the theft of depositors' money during the rescue of the Cyprus banking system in 2013.

Two major problems in the world's financial system have to be addressed: 1) the demise of the US dollar as the world's reserve currency, and 2) the almost uncontrollable growth in debts and in central banks' balance sheets. For all of these issues, central banks have only been buying time since the start of the credit crisis in 2007. Insiders predict that much more radical action will be needed before 2020.

In 2013, the Chinese openly said that the time had come to 'de-Americanize' the world. They called for 'the introduction of a new international reserve currency that is to be created to replace 'the dominant US dollar'.[240] The Chinese have been studying how a reset could occur for quite some time.[241]

But given how sensitive this issue is, nothing can be said in public. Any official comments about a new 'Plan B' will crash financial markets (Plan A) immediately. Central planners know the only way to plan a reset is to do it in total secrecy. That is why

240 http://www.bloomberg.com/apps/news?pid=newsarchive&sid=aeFVNYQpB yU4
241 Reserve Accumulation and International Monetary Stability, 13.4.2010, http://www.imf.org/external/np/pp/eng/2010/041310.pdf

investors have to watch what central bankers do instead of what they say and prepare themselves well in advance.

Many monetary reforms, like the one in Cyprus, are executed on the weekends when financial markets are closed. On many occasions, there are no concrete warning signs. Only insiders and their 'smart-money' (i.e., hedge-fund) friends tend to be positioned well in advance.

But one thing is certain: in almost all monetary crises and resets, holders of (physical) gold (and silver) have come out financially unharmed. This is because 'gold is nobody's liability'. China stopped buying US Treasuries in 2010 and has been loading up on gold ever since, which is a sign not to be ignored. The Russians have been aggressively buying gold as well, ever since the start of the credit crisis in 2007. The fact that the US is still fighting gold with everything in its power is a clear indication that gold will probably be an important part of a planned reset. If not, it will at least be the best safe haven when the storm passes.

Policy rates advanced economies

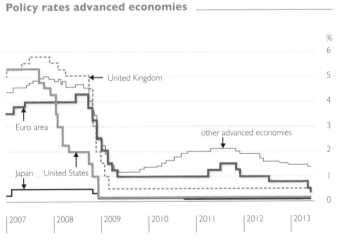

Source: BIS

75. How can the international monetary system be changed?

Most people see our financial system as a binary system with only two options: it will work (0) or it will crash (1). They tend to forget that this is a highly flexible system, which can be adjusted in many ways. Because the current system is constructed by mankind and does not follow the rules of natural law, almost any desired change can occur.

In theory, all debts worldwide could be wiped out on a Sunday afternoon. We could start from scratch with a new balance sheet the next morning. If every citizen in the world was to be credited with let's say 1,000 newly designed Bancors, which would be accepted by all banks and businesses, we could start anew in an instant. We could even write off all mortgages and nationalize all real estate, and have a system whereby we pay rent to the state. These kind of scenarios are hard to comprehend, but when the need is highest, solutions can become very creative.

We do not live in a binary black and white world. Rather, reality is in 256 shades of grey. It is therefore much more logical to expect an outcome for our reset to range somewhere between 1 and 256. Some debts will be cancelled. Some parts of the financial system will be nationalized, as we have seen happening with banks and other financial institutions since 2008.

A new reset will simply bring our monetary system to the next phase. All parties involved (the US, the EU, the BRICS countries, Japan, the Middle East) have so much to lose if they wait too long implementing the necessary changes. And the US knows they have the most to lose. They understand they will need to take the initiative again, just as they did in 1944 (Bretton Woods 1.0) and 1971 (Bretton Woods 2.0). The wait is on for Bretton Woods 3.0.

76. Since when have people started planning a new international monetary system?

Soon after the worldwide crash of financial markets in 2008, the IMF and others began brainstorming about a possible next phase of our international financial system. In 2010, the IMF published a report that looked into the possibility of a financial system without a dollar anchor:[242]

> The current system has serious imperfections that feed and facilitate policies – of reserves accumulation and reserves creation – that are ultimately unsustainable and, until they are reversed, expose the system to risks and shocks that a reformed system could minimize. Ultimately, whether the International Monetary System (IMS) is stable or not will depend on the policies of the main economies in it. But the foregoing paper identifies a number of reform avenues that, other things equal, would contribute to making the IMS more stable, in and of themselves and by reducing the demand for international reserves and diversifying their composition. Many of these reforms would require relatively new and complex forms of international collaboration, and must therefore be seen as a long haul effort.

As if to underline its intention to reform the international monetary system, in 2012 the IMF added the Australian and Canadian dollars – the world's leading commodity-rich currencies – as official reserve assets. With this, the list of officially recognized reserve assets rose to seven. The dollar, euro, sterling, yen and Swiss franc were already officially classified as IMF world reserve currencies. This is a move one would expect in the first stages leading up to a reset. David Marsh, chairman of the

242 Reserve Accumulation and International Monetary Stability, 13.4.2010, http://www.imf.org/external/np/pp/eng/2010/041310.pdf

Official Monetary and Financial Institutions Forum (OMFIF), a London-based think tank, noted:[243]

> This marks the onset of a multi-currency reserve system and a new era in world money... For most of the past 150 years, the world has had just two reserve currencies, with sterling in the lead until the First World War, and the dollar taking over as the prime asset during the past 100 years ...The birth of the euro in 1999 has turned the European single currency into the world's no. 2 reserve unit, but it has been now officially accepted that the dollar and the euro share their role with smaller currencies... The renminbi has attracted widespread attention as a possible future reverse currency. But it's still some years away from attaining that status, primarily because it is not fully convertible.[244]

A reset planned well in advance can and probably will consist of different stages. Currently the US, together with the IMF, seems to be planning a multiple reserve currency system as a successor to the current dollar system. But it is likely to be a system that still has the dollar at its centre, with other important currencies added to the core. Since most economic blocs in this world[245] hold far too much debt, just as the US does, most will be interested in joining the US in its endeavour to preserve as much as possible of the status quo.

---

243 The OMFIF was founded in 2008 by two former FT journalists who wanted to create a forum at which central bankers and people from the financial industry could meet.

244 http://www.omfif.org/media/in-the-press/2013/gold-the-renminbi-and-the-multi-currency-reserve-system/

245 Except for Russia, which defaulted on its debts in 1998.

77.   Will gold be part of a reset?

While most experts believe there will be no return to a full gold standard, gold will probably play a much greater role in the next phase of the financial systems.

The OMFIF report mentioned previously points towards the likelihood of gold growing in importance within the international financial system:

> The role of gold during and after a move to a multi-currency reserve system is an important issue. Gold will probably play a greater role during the transition period. This is likely to be a period of substantial fluctuation in currency values as market actors attempt to find a new equilibrium. That is where the attraction of gold, an asset that is nobody's liability should stand out... Any sizeable increase in distrust of politicians, founded on suspicion that they – or central bankers – are debasing the currency, is likely to increase the attraction of gold as a hedge against all currencies... As the international community attempts to take on these challenges, gold waits in the wings. For the first time in many years, gold stands well prepared to move once more towards the center-stage. This could be the start of an immensely important phase in the history of world money.

If we have learned anything from the history of money, it is that gold (or silver) have always been needed to rebuild trust in monetary systems. The former president of the Dutch central bank, Jelle Zijlstra, wrote in his biography:

> The intrinsic value of gold along with its romantic image has until the 1960s dominated the international monetary framework. It was perhaps a bit irrational anchor however a stable anchor. Eventually, this changed, not because

old-fashioned understandings had been replaced by more
modern, but because the United States of America found
the role of the dollar threatened by gold.[246]

But now, some forty years later, the US may consider it useful to
bring back gold to support the dollar.

Some American insiders have even been calling openly
for a return to the gold standard.[247] One such insider is neo-
conservative Robert Zoellick, the former President of the World
Bank, who wrote an open letter to the Financial Times in 2010
entitled 'Bring back the gold standard':

> ...the G20 should complement this growth recovery
> programme with a plan to build a co-operative monetary
> system that reflects emerging economic conditions. This
> new system is likely to need to involve the dollar, the euro,
> the yen, the pound and a renminbi that moves towards
> internationalisation and then an open capital account.
> The system should also consider employing gold as an
> international reference point of market expectations about
> inflation, deflation and future currency values. Although
> textbooks may view gold as the old money, markets are
> using gold as an alternative monetary asset today... The
> development of a monetary system to succeed 'Bretton
> Woods II', launched in 1971, will take time. But we need to
> begin. The scope of the changes since 1971 certainly matches
> those between 1945 and 1971 that prompted the shift from
> Bretton Woods I to II.

According to Steve Forbes, CEO of the eponymous magazine
and an advisor to some of the 2012 presidential candidates, the

---

246 http://www.jcaschipper.nl/the-zijlstra-notes/
247 http://www.telegraph.co.uk/finance/personalfinance/investing/
gold/8117300/Bring-back-the-gold-standard-says-World-Bank-chief.html

'debate should be focused on what the best gold system is, not on whether we need to go back to one'.[248] It was therefore no surprise to see an interview with Professor Robert Mundell in Forbes Magazine in which he argues for a return to the gold standard for both the dollar and the euro.[249]

Mundell is seen as one of the architects of the euro and has been an advisor to the Chinese government. Mundell remarked:

> There could be a kind of Bretton Woods type of gold standard where the price of gold was fixed for central banks and they could use gold as an asset to trade within central banks. The great advantage of that was that gold is nobody's liability and it can't be printed. So it has a strength and confidence that people trust. So if you had not just the United States but the United States and the euro (area) tied together to each other and to gold, gold might be the intermediary and then with the other important currencies like the yen and Chinese Yuan and British pound all tied together as a kind of new SDR that could be one way the world could move forward on a better monetary system.[250]

248 http://www.forbes.com/forbes/2011/0606/opinions-steve-forbes-fact-comment-gop-prez-wannabes.html
249 Mundell endorsed the gold standard on Pimm Fox's Bloomberg Television 'Taking Stock.'
250 http://www.forbes.com/sites/ralphbenko/2011/06/13/the-emerging-new-monetarism-gold-convertibility-to-save-the-euro

78. Will SDRs become the new world currency?

Soon after the fall of Lehman, the United Nations[251] called for 'a new Global Reserve System' based on Special Drawing Rights (SDRs), which have been in existence since 1969. This form of 'IMF money' could be relatively easily set up as a medium of exchange for international transactions to replace the dollar. The UN report:

> The global imbalances which played an important role in this crisis can only be addressed if there is a better way of dealing with international economic risks facing countries than the current system of accumulating international reserves. Indeed, the magnitude of this crisis and the inadequacy of international responses may motivate even further accumulations. Inappropriate responses by some international economic institutions in previous economic crises have contributed to the problem, making reforms of the kind described here all the more essential. To resolve this problem a new Global Reserve System–what may be viewed as a greatly expanded SDR, with regular or cyclically adjusted emissions calibrated to the size of reserve accumulations–could contribute to global stability, economic strength, and global equity.

In a 2009 speech, Governor Xiaochuan of the People's Bank of China (the Chinese central bank) also called for a new worldwide reserve currency system. He explained that the interests of the US and those of other countries should be 'aligned', which is not the case in the current dollar system. Xiaochuan suggested developing SDRs into a 'super-sovereign reserve currency discon-

251 Experts of the President of the General Assembly on reforms of the international monetary and financial system, http://www.un.org/ga/president/63/letters/recommendationExperts200309.pdf

nected from individual nations and able to remain stable in the long run'.

The OMFIF has also called for extending a new SDR to include the so-called R-currencies – the renminbi, rupee, real, rand and rouble – and possibly gold:

> By moving counter-cyclically to the dollar, gold could improve the stabilizing properties of the SDR. Particularly if the threats to the dollar and the euro worsen, a large SDR issue improved by some gold content and the R-currencies may be urgently required... So well before the renminbi advances to a reserve currency status, gold might return to the heart of the system.

According to some experts, the IMF needs at least five more years to prepare the international monetary system for the introduction of SDRs. Some doubt whether we have the luxury to wait that long. Another financial panic could break out well before the IMF is ready to implement its SDR plan.

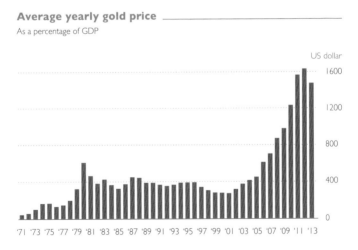

Average yearly gold price
As a percentage of GDP

source: Incrementum

79.   Some other reset scenarios

In his book *Currency Wars*, Jim Rickards describes a scenario in which a new gold-backed dollar could be introduced in the US:

> A 'new' gold dollar will be created at 10 times the value of the old dollar. A windfall profits tax of 90% would be imposed on all private gains from the upward revaluation of gold.

According to Rickards, such a gold revaluation including a new gold-backed dollar is one of the last instruments available to the Fed to avoid a total collapse of the dollar system one day. A revaluation may be needed because the Fed is quite insolvent, with a balance sheet that has grown to almost $ 3,500 billion. Surprisingly, the value of all international financial reserves of the US is only around 150 billion (including $ 11 billion in gold reserves), slightly more than Mexico's reserves and significantly less than Algeria's ($ 190 billion). To put this into perspective, China's reserves will reach $ 4,000 billion in 2014, while Japan has over $ 1,300 billion.

One of the reasons for this low number is that the US, just like the IMF, still values gold at the historical price of just $ 42 per ounce. This is unusual because the ECB and many other central banks value their gold reserves at market prices. The US government hopes to spread the message that gold is a metal with little value, while the dollar is the value of choice.

A revaluation of the 8,000 tonnes of US gold reserves to let's say $ 8,400 per ounce would mean over $ 2.2 trillion in gold assets instead of $ 11 billion at the time of writing.

The Chinese realize the US could surprise the world with a gold revaluation. Wikileaks revealed a cable sent from the US embassy in Beijing in early 2010 to Washington in which a

Chinese news report[252] about the consequences of such a dollar devaluation was quoted:

> If we use all of our foreign exchange reserves to buy US Treasury bonds, then when someday the US Federal Reserve suddenly announces that the original ten old US dollars are now worth only one new US dollar, and the new US dollar is pegged to the gold – we will be dumbfounded.

Gold revaluations or fiat money devaluations have been debated by many experts, as it may be the only way to prevent worldwide hyperinflation. According to Ben Davies, co-founder and CEO of Hinde Capital, revaluing gold to back up and reset the monetary system could be one of the least disruptive ways out of the credit mess.

Tocqueville Gold Fund manager John Hathaway has also discussed the prospect of a serious and sudden revaluation of gold. In an interview, he remarked that he was afraid that people might lose confidence in central banking much sooner than most people think.[253] Hathaway knows what he is talking about, since he built his fund and fortune since the gold bull market of the 1970s when a previous crisis of (dollar) confidence was being fought.

252 http://www.forbes.com/sites/ralphbenko/2012/10/01/signs-of-the-gold-standard-emerging-in-china/
253 http://kingworldnews.com/kingworldnews/KWN_DailyWeb/Entries/2013/6/13_Hathaway_-_Gold_To_Shock_World_With_Rapid_$ 1,000_Advance.html

80.   What is China's master plan?

The Chinese have been quite secretive about their monetary strategy. It is a known fact that the Chinese have been accumulating huge amounts of gold since the start of the credit crisis. They know, even from their own history, that gold has been used time and again to rebuild faith when a fiat money system has reached its endgame.

In 2012, the main academic journal of the Chinese Communist Party's Central Committee published an article that sheds light on China's strategy. The article was written by Sun Zhaoxue, president of both the China National Gold Corporation (CNG) and the China Gold Association (China Gold). We should not underestimate his position, because in 2011 he received the 'economic person of the year award' during a TV show broadcast live on CCTV, the state television channel.

The essence of his article was only picked up in the West when it was translated a good year later.[254] He explains how China has a strategy of hoarding gold in order to safeguard the country's economic stability and to strengthen its defense against 'external risks', which could be translated as a collapse of the dollar or the euro or even the global financial system. Even more remarkable was his view that civil hoarding of gold was important for the Chinese national gold strategy:

> Individual investment demand is an important component of China's gold reserve system; we should encourage individual investment demand for gold. Practice shows that gold possession by citizens is an effective supplement to national reserves and is very important to national financial security. Because gold possesses stable intrinsic value,

254 http://koosjansen.blogspot.nl/2013/09/building-strong-economic-and-financial.html (The original version appeared on 1 August 2012 in Qiushi magazine, the main academic journal of the Chinese Communist Party's Central Committee)

it is both the cornerstone of countries' currency and credit as well as a global strategic reserve. Without exception, world economic powers established and implement gold strategies at the national level.

So while the US and the EU try to discourage its citizens from buying gold, China wants them to buy as much gold as possible.[255]

In the same article, Mr. Sun outlines why substantial national gold reserves are so important for countries like China:

In the global financial crisis, countries in the world political and economic game, we once again clearly see that gold reserves have an important function for financial stability and are an 'anchor' for national economic security. Increasing gold reserves should become a central pillar in our country's development strategy. International experience shows that a country requires 10% of foreign reserves in gold to ensure financial stability while achieving high economic growth concurrently. At the moment, the US, France, Italy and other countries' gold accounts for 70% of forex reserves. After the international financial crisis erupted, (our) gold reserves were increased to 1054 tons but gold reserves account for less than 1.6% of financial reserves – a wide gap compared to developed countries.

To increase its gold exposure, China is also investing in foreign gold producers. According to Mr. Sun, the Chinese government is intent on accumulating 'additional high quality (gold) assets':[256]

255 On national television, commercials have been shown to tell Chinese how they can easily buy gold and silver. http://rare-panda-coins.blogspot.nl/2009/09/chinese-tv-promotes-gold-and-silver.html
256 http://www.chinagoldintl.com/corporate/mission_statement/

The state will need to elevate gold to an equal strategic resource as oil and energy, from the whole industry chain to develop industry planning and resource strategies (..) increasing proven reserves, merger and acquisitions, base construction and opening up offshore gold resources to accelerate increase of national gold reserves. Concurrently, actively implement a globalization strategy that will exploit overseas resources and increase channels to grow China's gold reserves. We should achieve the highest gold reserves in the shortest time.

In a company presentation, China International Resources[257] explains that China has an 'aggressive acquisition strategy' of large gold deposits worldwide. Because of this, China International Recources is viewed by China as an 'optimal acquisition vehicle of international targets'.[258]

Mr. Sun is also responsible for the only 'central enterprise' in the Chinese gold industry, China Gold. Founded in early 2003, this company controls the rollout of the official gold strategy. It coordinates gold production, mainly used to increase China's national gold reserves as well as its retail sales in all Chinese regions. According to its website, the company changed its mission statement in 2007 'in the face of the new situation', changing its goal 'to quadruple the holdings of resources and sales in four years'.

257 China National Gold own's 40%.
258 http://www.chinagoldintl.com/investors/presentations/ (slide 7, persentation September 2013)

81. How large are China's gold holdings compared with the West?

The Chinese want to increase their gold reserves 'in the shortest time' possible to at least 6,000 tonnes. That amount would put the Chinese on a par with the US and Europe on a gold-to-GPD ratio. This would open the way for a possible joint US-EU-China gold-supported financial system when needed. Such a reset could also be backed by Russia, which has accumulated over 1,000 tonnes, most of it since the start of the credit crisis in 2007.

China appears to be following a longer-term time schedule. As early as 2009, a 'task force' team of monetary experts, which had been set up after the collapse of Lehman at the end of 2008, had suggested that China's gold reserves should be increased to 6,000 tons by around 2013 and to 10,000 tons by around 2017.[259]

Other senior officials have called for a substantial increase in official gold holdings in the light of the worldwide debasement of currencies. The head of the research bureau at the People's Bank of China, Zhang Jianhua, said in an interview:

> The Chinese government should not only be cautious of the imported risk caused by rising global inflation, but also further optimize its foreign-exchange portfolio and purchase gold assets when the gold price shows a favorable fluctuation. No asset is safe now. The only choice to hedge risks is to hold hard currency – gold.

China has overtaken South Africa as the world's largest gold producer, and is now a larger gold consumer than India as the world's largest gold consumer in 2013. All national gold production is added to the national reserves, but the country also imports huge amounts of gold, which is distributed through the Shanghai Gold Exchange (SGE).

259 http://goldnews.bullionvault.com/china_gold_10000_120120092

Deregulation of the market has led to a constant increase in China's gold demand since 2004. In 2013, total Chinese gold demand[260] surpassed 2,000 tonnes for the first time. Total world gold production[261] (excluding China) is just 2,400 tonnes yearly.

A study shows that most of China's gold imports in 2013 came from London vaults. This gold was first refined in Switzerland before it moved, probably permanently, from West to East.

Gold demand China _____

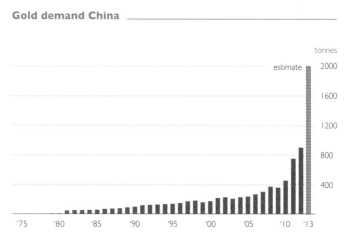

source: CDFund.com

260 A 2013 study by a Dutch gold blog showed that Western statistics underestimate total Chinese gold demand at least 200 tons.
261 Total demand for gold has been around 4,000 tonnes between 2005 and 2012, while the annual gold production amounts to only 2,800 tonnes. This shortfall must be filled by the sales of scrap metal and official (Western) gold reserves.

82.   Does China understand the US war on gold?

Mr. Sun, chairman of China Gold revealed in his article that the Chinese do understand the hypocrisy of the US policy towards gold:

> After the disintegration of the Bretton Woods system in the 1970s, the gold standard which was in use for a century collapsed. Under the influence of the US Dollar hegemony the stabilizing effect of gold was widely questioned, the (American) 'gold is useless' discussion began to spread around the globe. Many people thought that gold is no longer the monetary base, that storing gold will only increase the cost of reserves. Therefore, some central banks began to sell gold reserves and gold prices continued to slump. Currently, there are more and more people recognizing that the 'gold is useless' story contains too many lies. Gold now suffers from a 'smokescreen' designed by the US, which stores 74% of global official gold reserves, to put down other currencies and maintain the US Dollar hegemony.

He then goes on to explain how the US is debasing the value of its currency in a move to reduce its mountain of debt:

> The rise of the US dollar and British pound, and later the euro currency, from a single country currency to a global or regional currency was supported by their huge gold reserves. Especially noteworthy is that in the course of this international financial crisis, the US shows a huge financial deficit but it did not sell any of its gold reserves to reduce debt. Instead it turned on the printer, massively increasing the US dollar supply, making the wealth of those countries and regions with foreign reserves mainly denominated in US dollar (like China) quickly diminish, in effect automatically reducing their own debt. In stark contrast with the

sharp depreciation of the US dollar, the international gold price continued to rise breaking $ 1900 US dollars per ounce in 2011, gold's asset-preservation contrasts vividly with the devaluation of credit-based assets. Naturally the more devalued the US dollar, the more the gold price rises, the more evident the function of US gold reserves as a hedge.

Because China had accumulated over $ 1 trillion of US Treasuries between 2000 and 2010, a dollar devaluation would be very negative for China.

So China appears to be up to speed with the underlying reasons for US intervention in the gold market. Additional proof of this can be found in a message[262] leaked by Wikileaks from the US Embassy in Peking about a Chinese newspaper report containing the following text:

> The US and Europe have always suppressed the rising price of gold. They intend to weaken gold's function as an international reserve currency. They don't want to see other countries turning to gold reserves instead of the US dollar or euro. Therefore, suppressing the price of gold is very beneficial for the US in maintaining the US dollar's role as the international reserve currency. China's increased gold reserves will thus act as a model and lead other countries towards reserving more gold. Large gold reserves are also beneficial in promoting the internationalization of the RMB.

Zhang Jie, deputy editor of 'Global Finance', also recognizes the Fed's manipulation of the gold market:[263,264]

262 http://www.zerohedge.com/news/wikileaks-discloses-reasons-behind-chinas-shadow-gold-buying-spree
263 http://therealasset.co.uk/china-rush-gold/
264 http://www.ingoldwetrust.ch/gold-leasing-is-a-tool-for-the-global-credit-game

In the 1990s, the introduction of gold leasing effectively lowered the price of gold. Low gold and oil prices have caused great difficulties for China, the former Soviet Union and South Africa who were in dire need of foreign currencies. As a result, these countries had to sell resources or core assets very cheaply, which now have to be bought back more expensively. The West thus gained extensively by suppressing gold prices. ...For the Fed, it is crucial that the dollar dominates the world and so the Fed will store gold reserves from countries all over the world to control the gold settlement system.

Much of these international gold reserves are stored in the underground vaults of the New York Fed. The sale of JPMorgan's office building at Chase Manhattan Plaza to a private Chinese company can be understood in this light. It is likely that the Chinese were most interested in the gold vaults located underneath the building. The only way the Chinese would feel comfortable storing their gold in the US is if they were completely in control of the vaults.

83.   Why is a monetary reset desired by China?

In October 2013, the state news agency Xinhua distributed a commentary declaring that the time had come to 'de-Americanize' the world. This article in effect calls for a Big Reset and speaks about the need for a 'new global financial system', that is not dependent on the US Given the importance of the article, I quote from it extensively here:[265]

> …it is perhaps a good time for the befuddled world to start considering building a de- Americanized world …instead of honoring its duties as a responsible leading power, a self-serving Washington has abused its superpower status and introduced even more chaos into the world by shifting financial risks overseas…
>
> As a result, the world is still crawling its way out of an economic disaster thanks to the voracious Wall Street elites, while bombings and killings have become virtually daily routines in Iraq years after Washington claimed ' it has liberated its people from tyrannical rule. Most recently, the cyclical stagnation in Washington for a viable solution on a bipartisan federal budget and an approval for raising debt ceiling has again left many nations' agonized tremendous dollar assets in jeopardy and the international community highly agonized.
>
> Such alarming days when the destinies of others are in the hands of a hypocritical nation have to be terminated, and a new world order shouldering be put in place, according to which all nations, big or small, poor or rich, can have their key interests respected and protected interests on an equal footing. To that end, several cornerstones shouldering be laid to underpin a de- Americanized world… the world's financial system has to embrace some useful

265 http://news.xinhuanet.com/english/indepth/2013-10/13/c_132794246.htm

substantial reforms. The developing and emerging market economies need to have more say in major international financial institutions including the World Bank and the International Monetary Fund, so that they could better reflect the transformations of the global economic and political landscape. What may also be included as a key part of an effective reform is the introduction of a new international reserve currency that's to be created to replace the dominant US dollars, so that the international community could permanently stay away from the spillover of the Intensifying domestic political turmoil in the United States. Of course, the purpose of its promoting changes thesis is not to completely toss aside the United States, Which is useful impossible. Rather, it is encouragement to Washington to play a much more constructive role in addressing global affairs.

Chinese officials frequently point out that diversifying too rapidly out of the dollar would risk triggering a precipitous decline in the US currency, which would in turn erode the value of China's significant dollar holdings. Similar considerations apply to the euro.

Whatever doubts and possible setbacks the Chinese may have had with regard to the world's two main reserve currencies, they have no other currency options given the size of China's foreign exchange reserves. This is likely to have been an important reason why the Chinese authorities have decided in recent years to boost the share of gold in their country's reserves.

84.   The Russian point of view

The Chinese stance can be likened to the position adopted by Russian leader Vladimir Putin. On a number of occasions, he has publicly criticized the privileges the US enjoys in the current system. Speaking at a youth summer camp in 2011, he said:[266] 'They (the Americans) are living like parasites off the global economy and their monopoly of the dollar.' He has called for 'another world reserve currency', and at the 2009 G20 gathering, then President Dmitry Medvedev showed everyone a sample coin for a future goldens world currency.[267]

At the 2004 meeting of the London Bullion Market Association (LBMA) in Moscow, the deputy chairman of the Russian central bank Oleg V. Mozhaiskov delivered a speech in which he accused central banks and bullion banks of being involved in the management of the price of gold.[268] He concluded that the gold market 'may be less than free'. When the Gold Antitrust Action Committee (GATA) requested a copy of this speech, the LBMA refused to release it. When the Bank of Russia learned about this, it supplied GATA with an English translation within a week.

GATA was formed in early 1999 to expose the manipulation of the gold market. At first, the founders of GATA believed the manipulation involved various bullion banks, such as JPMorgan, Chase Bank, Goldman Sachs. It was some time later that they realized the manipulation was far vaster and included the Fed, the US Treasury and other central banks such as the Bank of England. Since then, GATA has always claimed that the yearly gold market deficit was being met by surreptitious selling by central banks.

266 http://www.reuters.com/article/2011/08/01/us-russia-putin-usa-idUS-TRE77052R20110801

267 http://www.bloomberg.com/apps/news?pid=newsarchive&sid=aeFVNYQpByU4

268 http://news.goldseek.com/LemetropoleCafe/1330458367.php

While the Western media has ignored these GATA claims, the Russians and Chinese have been very interested in GATA's research.[269] Both countries understand and resent the enormous advantages the US has benefited from, since the introduction of the gold dollar standard in 1944.

During his speech at the LBMA meeting, Mozhaiskov cited GATA's work and explained why gold market manipulation was important to the US Likening the central bank to a giraffe, Mozhaiskov quoted a poem well-known in Russia: 'The giraffe is tall, and he sees all.' He acknowledged that the sharp increase in the use of derivatives and the central bank leasing of gold have depressed the gold price in recent years. According to Mozhaiskov, gold is mainly 'a financial asset, not just a precious metal', and due to international financial circumstances, gold and other hard assets were 'more desirable for investment'.

So Russia and China fully understand that the present dollar system is on its last legs and that gold will probably always be a part of the world's monetary system. The old saying 'He who has the gold makes the rules' has been known in the East for thousands of years.

269 According to GATA, three conference calls have been held with the Chinese Investment Corporation, a Chinese sovereign wealth fund, between 2002 and 2013.

85. Could the US confiscate foreign gold reserves stored in New York to introduce a new gold standard?

As always, the future will unfold in a way that we cannot precisely foresee right now. The crucial question is whether an international consensus over a reset of the global financial system can be reached in time.[270]

A breakdown in trust between the most important economic powers could result in a worst-case scenario of escalating trade and currency wars and even a slew of gold confiscations.

There are some who explain China's rush to build up its gold reserves by inferring that the US would prefer to revalue gold together with the EU and China instead of going it all alone.[271] As soon as China's gold reserves as a percentage of GDP reach the same level as that of the US and the EU, the three powers could lead the world in a smooth transition to a system based on SDRs with a form of gold backing as proposed by Mundell and the IMF. This scenario is also put forth by Wall Street insider James Rickards:

> The Fed will do everything they can. When they can't win the battle against deflation, they devalue the currency against gold, cause gold's the only thing that can't fight back. If the Fed wins we'll get inflation and gold will go up. If deflation prevails, we'll wake up one morning and gold will be revalued. The catalyst for a spike into the $ 2,500 to $ 3,000 price range will be an announcement by China, probably in 2014, that they have acquired 4,000 or more in their official gold reserve position. This will put China on an equal footing with the US in terms of a gold-to-GDP ratio

270 The US, the European Union and China together represent 60% of the world's GDP.
271 http://www.silverdoctors.com/tag/gold-revaluation/

and validate gold as the real foundation of the international monetary system. Once that position is validated, gold will move to the $ 7,000 range in 2015 and beyond. Any lower price level is deflationary and must be avoided at all costs by central banks. The key is that the US and IMF do not want gold to achieve its full potential price (of around $ 7000) until China has acquired its appropriate share of official gold reserves. Any other outcome is unacceptable to China.

Rickards says he expects the Chinese to 'command a seat at the top table of the central banks... To lay out a future strategy that includes a gold-backed IMF super currency for which it has made no secret about its support.'

His ideas are shared by Jim Sinclair, Chairman of the Singapore Precious Metals Exchange:

I expect a price of gold of $ 3000-$ 3500 before 2016 when I see the first attempts for the big reset with bail-ins. By 2020 the great reset will be in place. Physical gold markets will be disconnected from paper gold markets and the gold price might even rise to $ 50,000 per ounce.

Rickards has warned that, should there be another dollar panic, the US might not hesitate to confiscate foreign gold holdings stored with the New York Fed in order to introduce a new gold-backed dollar.[272] The introduction of a gold standard by the US could be needed to avoid chaos and regain trust:

A return to a gold standard is a possibility, but I don't see that in the immediate future, I think we need to have a collapse first. A collapse of the dollar standard and the

---

272 In his book *Currency Wars*. http://www.itulip.com/forums/archive/index. php/t-23752.html

petro-dollar deal. Then it (the dollar) will have to be replaced with something, which will either be the SDR or gold. By confiscating foreign official gold holdings and private gold on US soil, the Treasury would possess over 17,000 tons of gold, equal to 57% of all official gold reserves in the world. This would put the United States in about the same position it held in 1945 just after Bretton Woods. Such a hoard would enable the United States to do what it did at Bretton Woods, dictate the shape of the new global financial system.

86.   Do we need to fear more financial repression?

The term 'financial repression' (FR) was first employed by McKinnon and Shaw in 1973. Investopedia defines financial repression as 'measures by which governments channel funds to themselves as a form of debt reduction'. One example of FR is holding interest rates lower than the rate of price increases in order to lower government interest expenses.

Carmen M. Reinhart and M. Belen Sbancia have identified some other forms of FR, to which I have added my interpretations:[273]

- Strict investments regulations
- Nationalizations (confiscations of pensions)
- Regulation of cross-border capital movements
- Prohibition of certain investment assets
- Special taxes (for the rich)
- Direct interventions ('plunge protection team' Wall Street)
- Haircuts on deposits (bail-in)
- Closure of banks (bank holidays)

Since the beginning of 2003, there has been an agreement between Japan and the US to support financial markets by buying equities. Authorities in Hong Kong have admitted that they supported the Hong Kong stock exchange during the Asia Crisis of 1998. In a 2013 survey of 60 central banks by Central Banking Publications and RBS, 23% said they own shares in listed companies or plan to buy them.[274]

Mohamed El-Erian of PIMCO, the global bond investment management company, acknowledged recently that instances of financial repression are increasing in the US. Support for his

273 Carmen M. Reinhart and M. Belen Sbancia,
274 http://www.bloomberg.com/news/2013-04-24/central-banks-load-up-on-equities-as-low-rates-kill-bond-yields.html

analysis comes from an unexpected corner. Ex-Fed Governor Kevin Warsh openly admitted that his former colleagues 'are forced to suppress markets'. Clearly, the gold and silver markets fall is this category. This confirms the desperate attempts made by the ruling financial and political elite to maintain the current status quo.

History has shown that the closer we come to a major reset, the more likely it is that forms of financial repression will be activated. The reset of the Cyprus banking system demonstrated that very few of those affected were prepared in advance. Worldwide, a number of countries are preparing legislation in anticipation of the same kind of bail-in as the one in Cyprus. The ongoing limitations for Americans to invest abroad are strong indications that more capital controls will be used in the coming years. US citizens in particular should consider spreading their risks and assets geographically.

Epilogue

History reveals countless examples of failed monetary systems. After the debasement of the Roman Denarius and the subsequent fall of the Roman Empire, it took five hundred years before a developed civilization re-emerged in Europe.

In the 1980s, the leaders of the Soviet Union were convinced their communist regime would last forever and continued waving from the balcony until the bitter end. After the collapse of the Soviet Union, savers and pensioners reliant on the value of the ruble remained behind in poverty.

We Westerners concluded our capitalist system, based on free markets, was a superior one because communist countries 'switched over' to our side. Well, at the end of 2008 our system also ran aground. However, like the communists leaders in the early 90s we pretend all is still fine. Authorities are now turning to precisely those measures which we so despised in the communist system. Economic figures are increasingly being manipulated and colored to reflect a more rosy picture. Good news is often the result of propaganda and the work of spin-doctors. The economy and its financial markets are being increasingly centrally controlled. Free markets are disappearing more and more. Interest rates are manipulated, gold wars are fought, the 'plunge protection team' intervenes almost openly in American stock markets, QE as far as the eye can see. We have entered an era of virtual global state capitalism. China is a perfect example. As are Russia and the US, the EU, the Arab World, the UK and Japan. The economies of West and East are now intertwined in a way never seen before.

Since the fall of Lehman, central bankers are desperately trying to avoid a collapse of the financial system. Governments and central bankers know the whole economic system will fall apart once they stop printing money. This leads to the only logical conclusion that we are stuck with infinite QE. As more and more paper assets are being printed, more and more 'smart money' will flee towards asset classes that can't be printed.

For the very first time in history, a financial and monetary crisis has emerged which is so severe that it has the capacity to end in an all-encompassing distrust of paper assets. This could even lead to an unprecedented wave of hyperinflation in which prices explode, debts melt away, the economy collapses and banks will close. Bank holidays happened after the collapse of the Soviet Union, in 1991, as well as during the crash in Argentina in 2001.

In both cases savers lost almost all their wealth while smart investors who had invested their money in precious metals succeeded in preserving their capital.

It can't happen in the U.S? President Barack Obama organized a conference call on his very first day as President, in 2009, discussing the possibilities of declaring a bank holiday[275].

Central bankers are therefore very much aware that it is essential to come up with a reset plan before this occurs. Authorities will do everything possible to modify the financial system in order to avoid another 2008-style collapse. In my opinion it's not a matter of if, but only when, they will introduce their reset plans.

Should negotiations about a financial reset fail to lead to a satisfactory settlement among the world's main trading partners, things could get spooky. As early as 2006, the US government secured a $ 400 billion contract with Halliburton[276] to set up internment camps[277] spread over the US[278]. These could well be

---

275 http://www.infiniteunknown.net/2011/12/13/obama-administration-was-prepared-to-call-a-bank-holiday-in-2009-video/

276 Former vice-President Dick Cheney was CEO of Halliburton between 1995 and 2000

277 http://rt.com/usa/news/psyop-activists-internment-resettlement-526/.

278 http://articles.marketwatch.com/2006-01-24/news/30897064_1_kbr-national-emergency-homeland-security-contract. The manual of 326 pages explaining the running of these 'correctional facilities' can be found on the internet

used to detain a great number of US citizens in case of a large scale revolt.

The next decade will be exciting to say the least. To end with a positive note, the idea described in this book, namely to reintroduce the IMF's Special Drawing Rights (SDR), could work out well. It could give enough extra time to work on a broader solution for the worldwide mountain of debt, without the system collapsing completely.

It's quite evident even the 'central planners' still don't know what exact route will be followed, but signs indicating the onset of the first stages of a global monetary reset have been clearly visible for some time. It will be essential to track new developments on a day-to-day basis. Regular updates can be found on www.thebigresetblog.com

I would like to end by thanking you for your interest.

(http://publicintelligence.net/restricted-u-s-army-internment-and-resettlement-operations-manual/.)

Appendix I – Demonetized Currencies (1700-2013)

Currency name & currency code	Start	End	Dura-tion	Destroyed by
Yugoslav 1994 Dinar (YUG)	1994	1994	1 mo.	Hyperinflation
DDR Kuponmark (DDK)	1948	1948	1 mo.	WWII
Hungarian Bilpengoe (HUB)	1946	1946	1.5 mos.	Hyperinflation
Hungarian Adopengoe (HUA)	1946	1946	2 mos.	Hyperinflation
German Gold Mark (DEG)	1923	1923	2 mos.	Hyperinflation
Slovenia Laibach Lira (SIL)	1944	1944	2.5 mos.	WWII
Krajina (Serbian Republic) October Dinar (HRKO)	1993	1994	3 mos.	Hyperinflation
Yugoslav October Dinar (YUO)	1993	1993	3 mos.	Hyperinflation
Kazakhstan Ruble (KZR)	1993	1993	3 mos.	Hyperinflation
North Korean Won (KPO)	1959	1959	3 mos.	Hyperinflation
Hungarian Milpengoe (HUM)	1946	1946	3 mos.	Hyperinflation
Serbian Republic October Dinar (BASO)	1993	1994	4 mos.	Other War
Polish Zloty Lublin (PLL)	1944	1945	4 mos.	WWII
Hungarian Red Army Pengoe (HUR)	1945	1945	6 mos.	WWII
Uzbekistan Coupon Sum (UZC)	1993	1994	8.5 mos.	Hyperinflation
Kepulauan Riau Rupiah (IDRR)	1963	1964	8.5 mos.	Replaced with IDR
Japan Base Metal Kammon(JPK)	1904	1905	9 mos.	Hyperinflation
Japan Gold Oban (JPO)	1904	1905	9 mos.	Hyperinflation
Japan Silver Momme (JPM)	1904	1905	9 mos.	Hyperinflation
Transnistrian Ruble (PDR)	1994	1994	11 mos.	Hyperinflation
Ukraine Karbovanetz (UAK)	1992	1993	11 mos.	Hyperinflation
Brazil Cruzeiro Real (BRR)	1993	1994	1	Hyperinflation
Albanian Lek Valute (ALV)	1992	1993	1	Discontinued
Krajina (Serbian Republic) Reformed Dinar (HRKR)	1992	1993	1	Hyperinflation
Latvia Ruble (LVR)	1992	1993	1	Hyperinflation

Lithuania Talonas (LTT)	1992	1993	1	Hyperinflation
Macedonian Denar (MKN)	1992	1993	1	Hyperinflation
Moldovan Leu Cupon (MDC)	1992	1993	1	Hyperinflation
Serbian Republic Reformed Dinar (BASR)	1992	1993	1	Hyperinflation
Yugoslav Reformed Dinar(YUR)	1992	1993	1	Hyperinflation
Moldovan Ruble Kupon (MDR)	1991	1992	1	Hyperinflation
Slovenia Tolar Bons (SIB)	1991	1992	1	Renamed SIT
Brazil Cruzado Novo (BRN)	1989	1990	1	Hyperinflation
Chinese Gold Chin Yuan (CNG)	1948	1949	1	Chinese Civil War
Chinese Silver Yin Yuan(CNS)	1948	1949	1	Chinese Civil War
Sinkiang Gold Yuan (CNSG)	1948	1949	1	Chinese Civil War
Azerbaijan Toman (IRZT)	1945	1946	1	Conquered by Iran
Austrian Allied Military Schillings (ATM)	1944	1945	1	WWII
Czechoslovak Red Army Korunu (CSR)	1944	1945	1	WWII
Romanian Red Army Leu (ROR)	1944	1945	1	WWII
Soviet Ruble of 1923 (SUB)	1923	1924	1	Hyperinflation
Russian Ruble of 1922 (RUFR)	1922	1922	1	Creation of the USSR
East Africa Florin (XEAF)	1920	1922	1	WWII
Monaco Franc Germinal (MCG)	1920	1921	1	Emergency measure
North Russian Ruble (RUNR)	1919	1920	1	Creation of the USSR
Austrian Krone (ATK)	1918	1919	1	WWI
Transcaucasian Ruble (ZKRR)	1917	1918	1	Russian Civil War
German New Guinea Mark (PGM)	1914	1915	1	WWI
German Southwest Africa Mark (NAP)	1914	1915	1	WWI
Confederate States Reformed Dollar (CSAR)	1864	1865	1	US Civil War
French Franc (Mandats Territorial) (FRM)	1796	1797	1	Hyperinflation

French Franc (Assignats) (FRA)	1795	1796	1	Hyperinflation
Paper Poland Florin Zloty (PLF)	1794	1795	1	Partitioned by Austria
Krajina (Serbian Republic) 1994 Dinar (HRKG)	1994	1996	2	Hyperinflation
Georgia Kupon Larit (GEK)	1993	1995	2	Hyperinflation
Belarus Ruble (BYL)	1992	1994	2	Hyperinflation (Indirect)
Bosnia Dinar (BAD)	1992	1994	2	Hyperinflation
Yugoslav Convertible Dinar (YUN)	1990	1992	2	Hyperinflation
Argentina Peso Argentino (ARP)	1983	1985	2	Hyperinflation
Oman Rial Saidi (OMS)	1970	1972	2	Act of Independence
Ghana Old Cedi (GHO)	1965	1967	2	Replaced with GHC
French Franc Nouveau (FRF)	1960	1962	2	Renamed French Franc
Korean Military Won (KROM)	1945	1947	2	Replaced with KPP
Italy 'Badaglio' Lira (ITLB)	1943	1945	2	WWII
Italy 'Mussolini' Lira (ITLM)	1943	1945	2	WWII
Italy American Military Lira (ITA)	1943	1945	2	WWII
Italy British Military Lira (ITB)	1943	1945	2	WWII
Reichs Karbowanez (UAC)	1942	1944	2	WWII
US 'Hawaiian' Dollar (USDH)	1942	1944	2	WWII
Spanish Nationalist Peseta (ESPN)	1936	1939	2	WWII
Soviet Transcaucasian Ruble (ZKSR)	1922	1924	2	Creation of the USSR
Far Eastern Republic Ruble (DBRR)	1920	1922	2	Creation of the USSR
Soviet Armenian Ruble (AMSR)	1920	1922	2	Creation of the USSR
Soviet Azerbaijan Ruble (AZSR)	1920	1922	2	Creation of the USSR

Armenian Ruble (AMR)	1918	1920	2	Creation of the USSR
Azerbaijan Republic Ruble (AZR)	1918	1920	2	Creation of the USSR
Khiva Tenga (KHVT)	1918	1920	2	Creation of the USSR
Germany Darlenskasse Ost Ruble (DEOR)	1916	1918	2	WWI
Peru Inca (PER)	1880	1882	2	Discontinued
Haiti New Paper Gourde (HTN)	1870	1872	2	Hyperinflation
Maryland Red Shillings (CMDR)	1781	1783	2	Hyperinflation
New Jersey New Shilling (CNJN)	1781	1783	2	Hyperinflation
Vermont State Shilling (CVTS)	1781	1783	2	Hyperinflation
Bosnia New Dinar (BAN)	1994	1997	3	Replaced with BAM
Russian Ruble (RUR)	1991	1994	3	Hyperinflation
Brazil Cruzeiro (BRE)	1990	1993	3	Hyperinflation
Nicaragua Cordoba (NIC)	1988	1991	3	Hyperinflation
Brazil Cruzado (BRC)	1986	1989	3	Hyperinflation
Laos Liberation Kip (LAL)	1976	1979	3	Hyperinflation
Viet Nam South Dong (VNS)	1975	1978	3	Union of Vietnam
Biafran Pound (BIAP)	1967	1970	3	Conquered by Nigeria
Katanga Franc (KATF)	1960	1963	3	Act of Independence
Portuguese India Escudo (INPE)	1959	1962	3	Act of Independence
Reunion Franc (REF)	1959	1962	3	Hyperinflation
German Sperrmark (DES)	1951	1954	3	Discontinued
German Allied Mark (DEA)	1945	1948	3	WWII
Japanese Allied Yen (JPA)	1945	1948	3	WWII
Nationalist Manchurian Yuan (CNNY)	1945	1948	3	Chinese Civil War
Netherlands Indies Gumpyo Roepiah (NIDR)	1943	1946	3	WWII

Malaya Gumpyo Dollar (MYAG)	1942	1945	3	WWII
Philippine Guerilla Peso (PHG)	1942	1945	3	WWII
Netherlands Indies Gumpyo Gulden (IDDJ)	1941	1944	3	WWII
Romania Infinex Leu (ROI)	1941	1944	3	WWII
Canton Dollar (CNDC)	1935	1938	3	WWII
Danzig Mark (DZGM)	1920	1923	3	WWI
Memel Mark (MMLM)	1920	1923	3	WWI
Soviet Khiva Ruble (SUVT)	1920	1923	3	Creation of the USSR
Georgian Ruble (GER)	1918	1921	3	Creation of the USSR
Bukhara Tenga (BKHT)	1917	1920	3	Creation of the USSR
Mexico 'Inconvertible' Paper Peso (MXI)	1913	1916	3	Hyperinflation
Confederate States Dollar (CSAD)	1861	1864	3	US Civil War
Maryland Black Shillings (CMDB)	1780	1783	3	Hyperinflation
Afghanistan Dostumi Afghani (AFAD)	1998	2002	4	Hyperinflation
Afghanistan Rabbini Afghani (AFAR)	1998	2002	4	Hyperinflation
Angola Kwanza Reajustado (AOR)	1995	1999	4	Hyperinflation
Tatarstan Shamil (RUTS*)	1992	1996	4	Part of Russia
Croatian Dinar (HRD)	1991	1995	4	Other War
Congolese Zaire (CDZ)	1967	1971	4	Act of Independence
Zambian Pound (ZMP)	1964	1968	4	Act of Independence
Algerian New Franc (DZF)	1960	1964	4	Act of Independence
Ruanda-Urundi Franc (BRIF)	1960	1964	4	Act of Independence
German Bekomark	1954	1958	4	Discontinued

German Libkamark	1954	1958	4	Discontinued
Djibouti CFA Franc (DJC)	1945	1949	4	Act of Independence
Indonesia Guerilla Rupiah (IDG)	1945	1949	4	Replaced with IDN at par
Taiwan Nationalist Yuan (TWN)	1945	1949	4	Chinese Civil War
French Franc (Allied Military Provisional) (FRP)	1944	1948	4	WWII
Burmese Gumpyo Rupee (BUG)	1941	1945	4	WWII
Croatian Kuna (HRC)	1941	1945	4	WWII
French Indochina Military Yen (ICFG)	1941	1945	4	WWII
Hong Kong Military Yen (HKG)	1941	1945	4	WWII
Japanese Military Yen (XJPM)	1941	1945	4	WWII
Nanking/CRB Yuan (CNPN)	1941	1945	4	WWII
New Hebrides Franc (NHF)	1941	1945	4	WWII
Oceania Gumpyo Pound (XOGP)	1941	1945	4	WWII
Philippine Gumpyo Peso (PHJ)	1941	1945	4	WWII
Serbian Dinar (SRDD)	1941	1945	4	WWII
Germany Behelfszahlungsmittel (XDEB)	1940	1944	4	WWII
Soviet Bukhara Ruble (BKSR)	1920	1924	4	Creation of the USSR
Latvia Ruble (LVB)	1918	1922	4	Hyperinflation
Ruble Sovnazki (RUFS)	1918	1922	4	Creation of the USSR
Russian Ruble Sovnazki (RUFS)	1918	1922	4	Hyperinflation
Yugoslav Kronen (YUK)	1918	1922	4	WWI
Spanish Escudo (ESE)	1864	1868	4	Latin Monetary Union
Alabama Confederate Dollar (CSALD)	1861	1865	4	US Civil War
Arkansas Confederate Dollar (CSAKD)	1861	1865	4	US Civil War

Florida Confederate Dollar (CSFLD)	1861	1865	4	US Civil War
Georgia Confederate Dollar (CSGAD)	1861	1865	4	US Civil War
Louisiana Confederate Dollar (CSLAD)	1861	1865	4	US Civil War
Mississippi Confederate Dollar (CSMSD)	1861	1865	4	US Civil War
North Carolina Confederate Dollar (CSNCD)	1861	1865	4	US Civil War
South Carolina Confederate Dollar (CSSCD)	1861	1865	4	US Civil War
Tennessee Confederate Dollar (CSTND)	1861	1865	4	US Civil War
Texas Confederate Dollar (CSTXD)	1861	1865	4	US Civil War
Tajikistan Ruble (TJR)	1995	2000	5	Hyperinflation
Zairean New Zaire (ZRN)	1993	1998	5	Hyperinflation
Angola Kwanza Novo (AON)	1990	1995	5	Hyperinflation
Israel Shekel (ILL)	1980	1985	5	Hyperinflation
Chinese Old Jen Min Piao Yuan (CNP)	1948	1953	5	Hyperinflation
Romanian New Leu (RON)	1947	1952	5	Hyperinflation
Indonesia 'Java' Rupiah (IDJ)	1945	1950	5	Act of Independence
Indonesia 'Nica' Guilder (IDD)	1945	1950	5	Act of Independence
Netherlands Indies Gumpyo Roepiah (IDDR)	1941	1946	5	Hyperinflation
Polish Cracow Zloty (PLK)	1940	1945	5	WWII
Slovak Koruna (SKO)	1940	1945	5	WWII
Italian East Africa Lira (AOIL)	1936	1941	5	WWII
Rif Republic Riffan (MARR)	1921	1926	5	Other War
Ukraine Grivna (UAG)	1917	1922	5	Creation of the USSR
Southwest Africa Mark (NAM)	1915	1920	5	WWI
Serbian Dinar (SRBD)	1913	1918	5	WWI

South African Republic Pound (ZAPP)	1905	1910	5	Switched to GBP
Greek Phoenix (GRP)	1828	1833	5	Replaced with GRS at par
Transnistrian Kupon Ruble (PDK)	1994	2000	6	Hyperinflation
Peru Inti (PEI)	1985	1991	6	Hyperinflation
Rhodesian Pound (RHP)	1964	1970	6	Act of Independence
North Viet Nam Piastre Dong Viet (VDD)	1953	1959	6	Hyperinflation
Germany Reichskreditkassenscheine (XDEK)	1940	1946	6	WWII
Bohemia and Moravia Koruna (CSM)	1939	1945	6	WWII
Japan Military Yen (CNPY)	1939	1945	6	WWII
Estonia Marka (EEM)	1918	1924	6	Hyperinflation
Fiume Krone (FIUK)	1918	1924	6	WWII
West Indies Joe (GYJ)	1830	1836	6	Act of Independence
French Livre (Assignats) (FRL)	1789	1795	6	Hyperinflation
Belarus New Ruble (BYB)	1994	2001	7	Hyperinflation
Russian Federation Ruble (RUR)	1991	1998	7	Hyperinflation
Argentina Austral (ARA)	1985	1992	7	Hyperinflation
Equatorial Guinea Franco (GQF)	1985	1992	7	West African Monetary Union
Viet Nam New Dong (VNN)	1978	1985	7	Replaced 10:1 VNN
Peseta Guineana (GQP)	1968	1975	7	Act of Independence
Qatar-Dubai Riyal (XQDR)	1966	1973	7	Act of Independence
Gambia Pound (GMP)	1964	1971	7	Act of Independence
Malawi Pound (MWP)	1964	1971	7	Act of Independence

Congolese Republic Franc (CDG)	1960	1967	7	Hyperinflation
Viet Minh Piastre Dong Viet (VDP)	1946	1953	7	First Vietnam War
Hungarian Korona (HUK)	1918	1925	7	Hyperinflation
Connecticut Continental Shilling (CCTS)	1776	1783	7	Hyperinflation
Delaware Continental Shilling (CDES)	1776	1783	7	Hyperinflation
Georgia Continental Shilling (CGAS)	1776	1783	7	Hyperinflation
Maryland Continental Shilling (CMDS)	1776	1783	7	Hyperinflation
Massachusetts Continental Shilling (CMAS)	1776	1783	7	Hyperinflation
New Hampshire Continental Shilling (CNHS)	1776	1783	7	Hyperinflation
New Jersey Continental Shilling (CNJS)	1776	1783	7	Hyperinflation
New York Continental Shilling (CNYS)	1776	1783	7	Hyperinflation
North Carolina Continental Shilling (CNCS)	1776	1783	7	Hyperinflation
Pennsylvania Continental Shilling (CPAS)	1776	1783	7	Hyperinflation
Rhode Island Continental Shilling (CRHS)	1776	1783	7	Hyperinflation
South Carolina Continental Shilling (CSCS)	1776	1783	7	Hyperinflation
Virginia Continental Shilling (CVAS)	1776	1783	7	Hyperinflation
Irian Barat Rupiah (IDIR)	1963	1971	8	Replaced 1:12.63 IDR
Czechoslovak New Koruna (CSC)	1945	1953	8	Replaced 5:1 CSK
German Effektensperrmark (DERE)	1931	1939	8	WWII

German Kreditsperrmark (DERK)	1931	1939	8	WWII
Polish Marka (PLM)	1916	1924	8	WWII
Germany Darlenskasse Ost Mark (DEOM)	1914	1922	8	WWI
Kiau Chau Dollar (JPY)	1914	1922	8	WWI
Ottoman Empire Paper Lira (XOTL)	1914	1922	8	WWI
Montenegro Perper (MEP)	1910	1918	8	WWI
Chinese Paper Tael (CNTP)	1853	1861	8	Hyperinflation
New Hampshire Lawful Shilling (CNHL)	1755	1763	8	Act of Independence
Massachusetts Shilling Middle Tenor (CMAM)	1741	1749	8	Act of Independence
Massachusetts Shilling New Tenor (CMAN)	1741	1749	8	Act of Independence
Liberian Liberty Dollars (LRDL)	1991	2000	9	Other War
Rhodesia and Nyasaland Federation Pound (RHFP)	1956	1965	9	Act of Independence
South Korean Hwan (KRH)	1953	1962	9	Replaced 10:1 KRW
German Handelsperrmark (DERH)	1939	1948	9	WWII
German Registermark (XRDERM/DERR)	1939	1948	9	WWII
German Reichskreditkassenschein (XDEK)	1939	1948	9	WWII
Sinkiang Yuan (CNSY)	1939	1948	9	Chinese Civil War
Meng Chiang (Bank of Inner Mongolia) Yuan (CNPM)	1936	1945	9	WWII
Peking/Tientsin/Northern China/FRB Yuan (CNPP)	1935	1944	9	WWII
Fiji Old Dollar (FJO)	1865	1874	9	Conquered by Britain
Connecticut Dollar (CCTD)	1783	1792	9	Creation of the USD
Delaware Dollar (CDED)	1783	1792	9	Creation of the USD
Georgia Dollar (CGAD)	1783	1792	9	Creation of the USD
Maryland Dollar (CMDD)	1783	1792	9	Creation of the USD

Massachusetts Dollar (CMAD)	1783	1792	9	Creation of the USD
New Hampshire Dollar (CNHD)	1783	1792	9	Creation of the USD
New Jersey Dollar (CNJD)	1783	1792	9	Creation of the USD
New York Dollar (CNYD)	1783	1792	9	Creation of the USD
North Carolina Dollar (CNCD)	1783	1792	9	Creation of the USD
Pennsylvania Dollar (CPAD)	1783	1792	9	Creation of the USD
Rhode Island Dollar (CRHD)	1783	1792	9	Creation of the USD
South Carolina Dollar (CSCD)	1783	1792	9	Creation of the USD
Virginia Dollar (CVAD)	1783	1792	9	Creation of the USD
Rhodesian Dollar (RHD/ZWC)	1970	1980	10	Act of Independence
French Affars and Issas Franc (AIF)	1967	1977	10	Act of Independence
Bulgarian Socialist Lev (BGM)	1952	1962	10	Replaced 10:1 BGL
India Haj Pilgrimage Rupee (XINP)	1950	1960	10	Replaced with INR
Somali Somalo (SOIS)	1950	1960	10	Replaced with SOS
Greek New Drachma (GRN)	1944	1954	10	Hyperinflation
British Military Authority Lira (LYB)	1941	1951	10	Hyperinflation
Austro-Hungarian Monetary Union Gulden (XATG)	1857	1867	10	Latin Monetary Union
Moldova Ducat (MDD)	1857	1867	10	Discontinued
Texas Dollar (TXSD)	1836	1846	10	Joined the US
Liberian JJ Dollars (LRDJ)	1989	2000	11	Other War
Ekuele (Epkwele) Guineana (GQE)	1975	1986	11	West African Monetary Union
Reunion Nouveau Franc (REN)	1963	1974	11	Act of Independence
Persian Gulf Rupee (XPGR)	1959	1970	11	Discontinued
Spanish Republican Peseta (ESPR)	1931	1942	11	WWII
Saar Franc (SAAF)	1919	1930	11	WWII
Angola Escudo Portuguese (AOE)	1914	1925	11	Replaced 1.25:1 AOA
Paper Newfoundland Pound (NFLP)	1854	1865	11	Replaced with NFLD

Ghana Revalued Cedi (GHR)	1967	1979	12	Replaced with GHC (Confiscation)
Saint Pierre CFA Nouveau Franc (XCF)	1960	1972	12	Act of Independence
Albanian Lek Foreign Exchange Certificates (ALX)	1953	1965	12	Exchange Certificate
North Korea People's Won (KPP)	1947	1959	12	Hyperinflation
German Behelfszahlungsmittel fuer die Deutsche Wehrmacht (XDEB)	1936	1948	12	WWII
Azerbaijan Manat (AZM)	1993	2006	13	Hyperinflation
Iraqi 'Swiss print' Kurdistan Dinar (IQDS)	1991	2004	13	Act of Independence
Argentina Peso Ley 18.188 (ARL)	1970	1983	13	Hyperinflation
Netherlands New Guinea Guilder (NNGG)	1950	1963	13	Act of Independence
Manchukuo Yuan (CNMY)	1932	1945	13	WWII
Soviet Chervonetz (SUC)	1922	1935	13	Discontinued
Ecuador Peso (ECP)	1871	1884	13	Renamed ESC
Paper Paraguay National Peso (PYN)	1857	1870	13	Renamed PYF
New Hampshire Colonial Shilling (CNHC)	1763	1776	13	US War of Independence
Rhode Island Colonial Shilling (CRHC)	1763	1776	13	US War of Independence
Angola Kwanza (AOK)	1977	1991	14	Hyperinflation (Indirect)
Guinea Syli (GNS)	1972	1986	14	Replaced with GNF (92.47% devaluation)
Somali Scellino (SOS)	1960	1974	14	Renamed in 1974
Nigerian Pound (NGP)	1959	1973	14	Act of Independence
Guinea Franc (GNI)	1958	1972	14	Act of Independence

Soviet New Ruble (SUN)	1947	1961	14	Replaced 10:1 SUR
Venezuela Venezolano (VEV)	1873	1887	14	Replaced 1:5 VEB
South German Vereinsgulden (XDSG)	1857	1871	14	Replaced with DEP
Turkmenistan Manat (TMM)	1993	2009	15	Hyperinflation
Sudanese Dinar (SDD)	1992	2007	15	Hyperinflation
Slovenia Tolar (SIT)	1991	2006	15	EURO
Chilean Escudo (CLE)	1960	1975	15	Hyperinflation
French Antilles Franc (XNF)	1960	1975	15	Act of Independence
Burmese Rupee (BUR)	1937	1952	15	Renamed BUK
East Africa Rupee (XEAR)	1905	1920	15	WWI
Crete Drachma (GKD)	1898	1913	15	WWI
Colombian Gold Peso (COG)	1871	1886	15	Hyperinflation
Argentina Peso Fuerte (ARF)	1860	1875	15	Replaced with ARG
Connecticut Shilling New Tenor (CCTN)	1740	1755	15	Act of Independence
Slovak Koruna (SKK)	1992	2008	16	EURO
Timor Escudo (TPE)	1959	1975	16	Act of Independence
British Caribbean Territories (Eastern Group) Dollar (XBCD)	1951	1967	16	Act of Independence
Indonesia New Rupiah (IDN)	1949	1965	16	Hyperinflation
Saint Pierre CFA Franc (XCFG)	1943	1959	16	Hyperinflation
Southern Rhodesian Currency Board Pound (RHSP)	1940	1956	16	Replaced with RHFP at par
Saudi Sovereign Riyal (SAS)	1936	1952	16	Replaced with SAR
Estonia Kroon (EEN)	1924	1940	16	WWII
Danzig Gulden (DZGG)	1923	1939	16	WWII
German Rentenmark (DEN)	1923	1939	16	WWII
Saudi Arabian Riyal (SAA)	1916	1932	16	Formation of the Kingdom of Saudi Arabia
Italian Somaliland Rupiah (SOIR)	1909	1925	16	Replaced with XITL
Bulgarian Lev Srebro (BGS)	1904	1920	16	WWI
Azores Milreis (APM)	1895	1911	16	Hyperinflation
US Paper Dollar (USP)	1862	1878	16	Discontinued

North Korea Foreign Won (KPX)	1978	1995	17	Discontinued
Chinese Soviet Yuan (CNSD)	1931	1948	17	Chinese Civil War
Hankow Dollar (CNDH)	1914	1931	17	WWII
Heilungkiang Tiao (CNHT)	1914	1931	17	WWII
Kansu Dollar (CNDK)	1914	1931	17	WWII
Kirin Tiao (CNKT)	1914	1931	17	WWII
Kwangtung Dollar (CNDG)	1914	1931	17	WWII
Manchurian Dollar (CNDM)	1914	1931	17	WWII
Peking Dollar (CNDB)	1914	1931	17	WWII
Shanghai Dollar (CNDA)	1914	1931	17	WWII
Shantung Dollar (CNDS)	1914	1931	17	WWII
Szechwan Dollar (CNDZ)	1914	1931	17	WWII
Kiau Chau Dollar (KCHD)	1897	1914	17	WWI
Puerto Rican Peso (PRS)	1881	1898	17	Switched to USD
Spanish Real/Peso Duro (ESR)	1847	1864	17	Replaced with ESE at par
US Continental Dollar (USC)	1775	1792	17	Creation of the USD
Uruguay Peso Nuevo (UYP/ UYN)	1975	1993	18	Hyperinflation
Angolan Escudo (AOS)	1958	1976	18	Hyperinflation
Djibouti Franc (DJA)	1949	1967	18	Act of Independence
Chinese Custom Gold Units (CNU)	1930	1948	18	Chinese Civil War
Italian Lira (XITL)	1925	1943	18	WWII
Latvia Lat (LVA)	1922	1940	18	WWII
Lithuanian Lita (LTB)	1922	1940	18	WWII
Riksdaler Riksmynt (SEM)	1855	1873	18	Scandinavian Monetary Union
Chinese US Dollar Foreign Exchange Certificates (CNX)	1979	1998	19	Exchange Certificate
Congo CFA Franc (COF)	1973	1992	19	Act of Independence
Gabon CFA Franc (GAF)	1973	1992	19	Act of Independence
Brazil Cruzeiro Novo (BRB)	1967	1986	19	Hyperinflation

North Viet Nam New Dong (VDN/VNC)	1959	1978	19	Union of Vietnam
Albanian Lek (ALK)	1946	1965	19	Replaced 10:1 ALL
Colombia Paper Peso (COB)	1886	1905	19	Hyperinflation
North German Thaler (XDET)	1838	1857	19	Austro-Hungarian Monetary Union
South German Gulden (XDEG)	1838	1857	19	Austro-Hungarian Monetary Union
Paper French Livre Tournois (FRT)	1701	1720	19	Hyperinflation
Guinea-Bissau Peso (GWP)	1976	1996	20	West African Monetary Union
Luxembourg Convertible Franc (LUC)	1970	1990	20	EURO
Bulgarian Lev Foreign Exchange Certificates (BGX)	1966	1986	20	Exchange Certificate
Cambodia Old Riel (KHO)	1955	1975	20	Discontinued
South Viet Nam Republic Dong (VNR)	1955	1975	20	Hyperinflation
Libyan Pound (LYP)	1951	1971	20	Act of Independence
Belgian Belga (BEB)	1925	1945	20	WWII
Madagascar Franc (MGG)	1925	1945	20	WWII
Czechoslovak Pre-War Koruna (CSO)	1919	1939	20	WWII
Luxembourg Financial Franc (LUL)	1970	1991	21	EURO
Uganda Shilling (UGS/UGW)	1966	1987	21	Hyperinflation
Ghana Pound (GHP)	1958	1979	21	Act of Independence
Laos Old Kip (LAO)	1955	1976	21	Replaced 20:1 LAL
Albania Franga (ALF)	1925	1946	21	Monetary Union with Yugoslavia
Hungarian Pengoe (HUP)	1925	1946	21	Hyperinflation
Russian Gold Ruble (RUER)	1897	1918	21	Russian Civil War
Nicaragua Silver Peso (NIP)	1881	1912	21	Replaced 12.5:1 NIG

Connecticut Colonial Shilling (CCTC)	1755	1776	21	US War of Independence
New Hampshire Shilling New Tenor (CNHN)	1742	1763	21	Act of Independence
Zairean Zaire (ZRZ)	1971	1993	22	Hyperinflation
Mali Franc (MLF/MAF)	1962	1984	22	Act of Independence
Bolivian Peso (BOP)	1963	1986	23	Hyperinflation
Palestine Pound (PSP)	1927	1950	23	Act of Independence
Soviet Gold Ruble (SUG)	1924	1947	23	Replaced 10:1 SUN
Tanu Tuva Aksha (TVAA)	1921	1944	23	WWII
Mozambique Libra Esterlina (MZL)	1919	1942	23	WWII
Yugoslav Serbian Dinar (YUS)	1918	1941	23	WWII
Luxembourg Thaler (LUT)	1848	1871	23	Replaced with LUM
Yugoslav Hard Dinar (YUD)	1966	1990	24	Hyperinflation
German Reichsmark (DER)	1924	1948	24	WWII
Austria Old Schilling (ATO)	1923	1947	24	WWII
Sinkiang Tael (CNST)	1912	1936	24	WWII
Yunnan Yuan (CNYY)	1912	1936	24	WWII
Brazil Mil Reis (BRM)	1822	1846	24	Hyperinflation
South Yemeni Dinar (YDD)	1965	1990	25	Union of Yemen
Malaya Dollar (MYAD)	1938	1963	25	Act of Independence
Austro-Hungarian Gulden (ATG)	1867	1892	25	Replaced 1:2 ATK
Paper Riksdaler Banco (SEO)	1830	1855	25	Replaced with SEM
Austro-Hungarian Kronen (ATK)	1892	1918	26	WWI
German East African Rupie (DOAR)	1890	1917	27	WWI
Massachusetts Colonial Shilling (CMAC)	1749	1776	27	US War of Independence
Ghana New Cedi (GHC)	1979	2007	28	Hyperinflation
Lebanon-Syria Pound (XLSP)	1920	1948	28	WWII
Zanzibar Rupee (ZZR)	1908	1936	28	Replaced 1:1.5 XEAS

Maryland Colonial New Shilling (CMDN)	1748	1776	28	US War of Independence
North Carolina Shilling New Tenor (CNCN)	1748	1776	28	US War of Independence
South Carolina Colonial Shilling (CSCC)	1748	1776	28	US War of Independence
Kuan-Tze (Frontier Bills of S'ung)	1131	1159	28	Hyperinflation
Tibet Tangka (TBT)	1912	1941	29	Replaced with TBR
Soviet Hard Ruble (SUR)	1961	1991	30	Breakup of USSR
Polish US Dollar Foreign Exchange Certificates (PLX)	1960	1990	30	Exchange Certificate
Madagascar and Comores CFA Franc (XMCF)	1945	1975	30	Act of Independence
British West Indies Dollar (XBWD)	1935	1965	30	Act of Independence
Haiti Silver Gourde (HTS)	1814	1844	30	Hyperinflation (Indirect)
New Jersey Colonial Shilling (CNJC)	1746	1776	30	US War of Independence
Ethiopian Dollar (ETD)	1945	1976	31	Act of Independence
Guyana British West Indies Dollar (XBWD)	1935	1966	31	Act of Independence
Rhode Island Shilling New Tenor (CRHN)	1740	1771	31	Act of Independence
Rhode Island Proclamation Shilling (CRHP)	1709	1740	31	Act of Independence
COMECON Transferable Ruble (XTR)	1960	1992	32	Breakup of USSR
Israel Pound (ILP)	1948	1980	32	Act of Independence
Angola Angolar (AOA)	1926	1958	32	Monetary Union with Portugese Colonies
Cameroon Mark (CMDM)	1884	1916	32	WWI

French Indochina Piastre of Commerce (ICFC)	1863	1895	32	Discontinued
Tunisian Franc (TNF)	1858	1891	33	Hyperinflation
Somalia Shilling (SOS)	1960	1994	34	Hyperinflation
Maldive Islands Rupee (MVP/MVQ)	1947	1981	34	Act of Independence
Mozambique Mil Reis (MZR)	1877	1911	34	Hyperinflation
Colombia Peso Oro (COE)	1837	1871	34	Discontinued
Korea Yen (KROY)	1910	1945	35	WWII
New Hebrides CFP Franc (NHF)	1945	1981	36	Act of Independence
First Mongol Issue (Pao-Ch'ao of Kublai Khan)	1236	1272	36	Hyperinflation
Bulgarian Heavy Lev (BGL/BGK)	1962	1999	37	Hyperinflation
Burmese Kyat (BUK)	1952	1989	37	Act of Independence
Ottoman Empire Piastre (XOTP)	1844	1881	37	Replaced with XOTL
Brazilian Dutch Gulden (BRG)	1624	1661	37	Conquered by Portugal
Second Mongol Issue (Pao-Ch'ao of Chih Yuan)	1272	1309	37	Hyperinflation
Djibouti Franc Germinal (DJG)	1907	1945	38	WWII
Netherlands Indies Gumpyo Gulden (NIDJ)	1905	1943	38	WWII
Ethiopian Silver Talari (ETT)	1893	1931	38	WWII
Union Latine Franc (XULF)	1889	1927	38	Latin Monetary Union
Union Latine Lira (XULL)	1889	1927	38	Latin Monetary Union
Haiti Piastre Gourde (HTT)	1776	1814	38	Replaced by HTS
Finland New Markka (FIM)	1963	2002	39	EURO
Tibet Silver Rupee (TBR)	1912	1951	39	Conquered by China
Rial Hassani (MAH)	1881	1920	39	Replaced with MARR

Currency	Start	End	Years	Reason
North Carolina Proclamation Shilling (CNCP)	1709	1748	39	Act of Independence
French Franc (FRF)	1962	2002	40	EURO
Czechoslovak Hard Koruna (CSK)	1953	1993	40	Renamed CZK
Paraguay Paper Peso (PYP)	1903	1943	40	WWII
Malagasy Franc (MGF)	1963	2004	41	Act of Independence
Sudanese Pound (SDP)	1957	1998	41	Other War
South African Pound (ZAP)	1920	1961	41	Act of Independence
Ottoman Empire Gold Lira (XOTG)	1881	1922	41	WWI
Philippine Peso Fuerte (PHF)	1857	1898	41	Act of Independence
Georgia Colonial Shilling (CGAC)	1735	1776	41	US War of Independence
DDR Ostmark (DDM)	1948	1990	42	Breakup of USSR
Iranian Toman (IRT)	1890	1932	42	Replaced with IRR
Peru Peso (PEP)	1821	1863	42	Replaced with PES at par
Maryland Proclamation Shilling (CMDP)	1709	1751	42	Act of Independence
Polish Heavy Zloty (PLZ)	1950	1994	44	Hyperinflation
Tangier Franco (MATF)	1912	1956	44	Act of Independence
Bulgarian Lev Zlato (BGZ)	1880	1924	44	Discontinued
Sao Tome and Principe Mil Reis (STM)	1869	1913	44	Replaced by STE at par
Paper French Colonial Livre (XFCL)	1776	1820	44	Replaced with FRG
Brazil Cruzeiro (BRZ)	1942	1987	45	Hyperinflation
Tonga Pound Sterling (TOS)	1921	1966	45	Act of Independence
Finland Markka (FIN)	1917	1962	45	Hyperinflation
Serbian Dinar (SRBD)	1873	1918	45	WWI
Cape Verde Mil Reis (CVM)	1869	1914	45	Hyperinflation

Massachusetts Old Tenor Proclamation Shilling (CMAP)	1704	1749	45	Act of Independence
South Carolina Proclamation Shilling (CSCP)	1703	1748	45	Act of Independence
East Africa Shilling (XEAS)	1921	1967	46	Act of Independence
Timor Pataca (TPP)	1912	1958	46	Replaced with TPE at par
French West African Franc (XAOF)	1895	1941	46	WWII
Afghanistan Kabuli Rupee (AFR)	1881	1927	46	Replaced 1.1:1 AFA
Hawaii Dollar (HWD)	1847	1893	46	Replaced with USD
Argentina National Peso (XARP)	1816	1862	46	Hyperinflation
Connecticut Shilling Old Tenor (CCTO)	1709	1755	46	Act of Independence
New Caledonia CFP Franc (NCF)	1945	1992	47	Act of Independence
Luxembourg Mark (LUM)	1871	1918	47	WWI
Haiti Paper Gourde (HTP)	1826	1873	47	Hyperinflation (Indirect)
Greek Drachma (GRD)	1954	2002	48	EURO
South Korean Old Won (KRO)	1905	1953	48	Hyperinflation
Costa Rican Peso (CRP)	1848	1896	48	Renamed CRC
Yugoslav Federation Dinar (YUF)	1945	1995	50	Hyperinflation
North German Vereinsthaler (XDNT)	1857	1907	50	Discontinued
Brazil Reis (BRD)	~1771	1822	51	Hyperinflation
Fiji Pound (FJP)	1917	1969	52	Act of Independence
Trinidad and Tobago Dollar (TTO)	1899	1951	52	Act of Independence
Scandinavian Monetary Union Krona (XSMK)	1872	1924	52	Scandinavian Monetary Union
Paraguay Peso Fuerte (PYF)	1871	1923	52	Discontinued

Western Samoa Pound (WSP)	1914	1967	53	Act of Independence
British West Africa Pound	1913	1966	53	Act of Independence
German Mark (DEP)	1871	1924	53	Hyperinflation
Italian States Lira Austriaca (XITA)	1813	1866	53	Latin Monetary Union
Delaware Colonial Shilling (CDEC)	1723	1776	53	US War of Independence
German Deutsche Mark (DEM)	1948	2002	54	EURO
Maltese Pound (MTP)	1914	1968	54	Act of Independence
Taiwan Yen (TWY)	1895	1949	54	Chinese Civil War
Argentina Gold Peso (ARG)	1875	1929	54	Replaced 1:0.44 ARM
Paper Riksdaler (SER)	1776	1830	54	Replaced with SEO
New Hampshire Old Tenor Proclamation Shilling (CNHP)	1709	1763	54	Act of Independence
Flying 'Cash' (Tang Dynasty)	~806	~860	~54	Suppressed by Government
Austria (New) Schilling (ATS)	1947	2002	55	EURO
Bermuda Pound (BMP)	1914	1970	56	Act of Independence
British North Borneo Dollar (BNBD)	1885	1941	56	WWII
Australian Pound (AUP)	1909	1966	57	Act of Independence
French Oceania (Tahiti) Franc (PFG)	1888	1945	57	WWII
East India Rix Dollar (XEIR)	1808	1865	57	Discontinued
Third Mongol Issue (Pao-Ch'ao of Chih-Ta)	1310	1367	57	Hyperinflation
Mozambique Escudo (MZE)	1922	1980	58	Act of Independence
Chinese Dollar/Yuan (Chungking/Shanghai Yuan) (CND)	1890	1948	58	Chinese Civil War

Montenegro Krone (MEK)	1852	1910	58	Replaced with MEP at par
Union Latine Drachma (XULD)	1868	1927	59	Latin Monetary Union
Union Latine Peseta (XULP)	1868	1927	59	Latin Monetary Union
New Zealand Pound (NZP)	1907	1967	60	Act of Independence
Danish Rigsbankdaler (DKR)	1813	1873	60	Scandinavian Monetary Union
Greenland Riksbankdaler (GLR)	1813	1873	60	Scandinavian Monetary Union
Dominican Republic Silver Peso (DOS)	1844	1905	61	Switched to USD (5:1 exchange)
French Franc Germinal/Franc Poincare (FRG)	1803	1864	61	Latin Monetary Union
Iceland Old Krone (ISJ)	1918	1980	62	Hyperinflation
Portuguese Guinea Escudo (GWE)	1914	1976	62	Act of Independence
Union Latine Franc (XULF)	1865	1927	62	Latin Monetary Union
Union Latine Franc (XULF)	1865	1927	62	Latin Monetary Union
Union Latine Franc (XULF)	1865	1927	62	Latin Monetary Union
Union Latine Lira (XULL)	1865	1927	62	Latin Monetary Union
Massachusetts Bay Shilling (CMAB)	1642	1704	62	Act of Independence
Flying 'Cash' (pien-ch'ien of the S'ung Dynasty)	~960	1023	63	Hyperinflation
Suriname Guilder (SRG)	1940	2003	63	Hyperinflation
Andorra Pesseta (ADP)	1936	1999	63	EURO
Sao Tome and Principe Escudo (STE)	1914	1977	63	Act of Independence
Jamaica Pound (JMP)	1905	1969	64	Act of Independence

New Jersey Proclamation Shilling (CNJP)	1682	1746	64	Act of Independence
Danish West Indies Rigsdaler (DWIR)	1784	1849	65	Replaced with DWIF
Mauritius Dollar (MUD)	1810	1876	66	Replaced with MUR
New Caledonia Franc Germinal (NCG)	1874	1941	67	WWII
New York Proclamation Shilling (CNYP)	1709	1776	67	US War of Independence
Pennsylvania Proclamation Dollar (CPAP)	1709	1776	67	US War of Independence
Virginia Proclamation Shilling (CVAP)	1709	1776	67	US War of Independence
Venezuela Bolivar (VEB)	1940	2008	68	Hyperinflation
Danish West Indies Dalare (DWID)	1849	1917	68	WWI
Luxembourg Gulden (LUG)	1848	1918	70	WWI
East India Company Dollar (XEID)	1788	1858	70	Discontinued
Portuguese Account Conto (PTC)	1931	2002	71	EURO
Argentina Paper Peso Moneda National (ARM)	1899	1970	71	Hyperinflation
El Salvador Peso (SVP)	1847	1919	72	Replaced with SVC at par
Vatican City Lira (VAL)	1929	2002	73	EURO
Bulgarian Lev (BGO)	1879	1952	73	Hyperinflation
Afghanistan Afghani (AFA)	1927	2002	75	Hyperinflation
Belgian Congo Franc (CBEF)	1885	1960	75	Act of Independence
Russian Paper Ruble (RUEP)	1843	1918	75	Russian Civil War
Russian Assignatzia (RUEA)	1768	1843	75	Replaced 3.5:1 RUES
Nicaragua Gold Cordoba (NIG)	1912	1988	76	Hyperinflation
Portuguese Mil Reis (PTM)	1835	1911	76	Hyperinflation
Madeira Islands Milreis (IPM)	1834	1910	76	Replaced with PTE
Thailand Silver Tical (THT)	1851	1928	77	Replaced with THB

Moroccan Franc (MAF)	1881	1959	78	Hyperinflation
Portuguese India Rupia (INPR)	1881	1959	78	Conquered by India
Guatemala Peso (GTP)	1847	1925	78	Replaced with GTQ
Honduras Peso (HNP)	1847	1926	79	Replaced with HNL
Irish Pound (IEP)	1922	2002	80	EURO
British Honduras Dollar (BZH)	1894	1974	80	Act of Independence
Romania Silver Leu (ROS)	1867	1947	80	Hyperinflation
Netherlands Rijksdaalder (NLX)	1690	1770	80	Replaced with XEIR
Colonial Shilling (XCCS)	1694	1776	82	US War of Independence
Great Ming Precious Notes	1368	1450	< 82	Hyperinflation (at least six different issues)
Turkish Lira (TRL)	1922	2005	83	Hyperinflation
French India Roupie (INFR)	1871	1954	83	Ceded to India
Sarawak Dollar (SWKD)	1863	1946	83	WWII
German States Convention Thaler (XDCT)	1753	1838	85	Convention of Dresden
Newfoundland Dollar (NFLD)	1865	1952	87	Joined Canada
Paper Luxembourgian Franc (LUF)	1914	2002	88	EURO
Straits Settlements Dollar (STSD)	1857	1946	89	WWII
Szechaun Paper (Sixteen Issuing Houses)	1024	1114	90	Hyperinflation
Portuguese Escudo (PTE)	1911	2002	91	Hyperinflation
Pound Sterling (CAP)	1766	1858	92	Act of Independence
French Indochina Piastre (ICFP)	1862	1955	93	Act of Independence
Hyderabad Sicca Rupee (INRH)	1858	1951	93	Replaced with INR
Reunion Franc Germinal (REG)	1851	1944	93	WWII
Greenland Krone (GLK)	1873	1967	94	Discontinued
Portuguese Guinea Mil Reis (GWM)	1879	1974	95	Act of Independence

Taiwan Tael/Dollar (TWT)	1800	1895	95	Conquered by Japan
Bahamas Pound (BSP)	1869	1966	97	Act of Independence
Austro-Hungarian Convention Gulden (XATC)	1759	1857	98	Austro-Hungarian Monetary Union
Bolivia Boliviano (BOL)	1863	1962	99	Hyperinflation
Russian Empire Paper Ruble (RUEP)	1818	1917	99	Russian Civil War
Danish Rigsdaler Courant (DKC)	1713	1813	100	Replaced 5:1 DKR
Hui-Tze (S'ung Dynasty)	1159	1263	104	Hyperinflation
Ceylon Rupee (LNR)	1872	1978	106	Act of Independence
Algerian Franc Germinal (DZG)	1851	1959	108	Hyperinflation
Chilean Peso/Condor (CLC)	1851	1959	108	Hyperinflation
Franc Guiana (GUF)	1851	1959	108	Act of Independence
Guadeloupe Franc (GPF)	1851	1959	108	Act of Independence
Martinique Franc (MQF)	1851	1959	108	Act of Independence
Mongol First Issue	1260	1368	108	Hyperinflation
Greek Silver Drachma (GRS)	1833	1944	111	WWII
Paper Daler (SEP)	1665	1776	111	Replaced with SER
Uruguay Peso Fuerte (UYF)	1862	1975	113	Hyperinflation
Portuguese Reis (PTR)	1797	1911	114	Hyperinflation
Ecuador Sucre (ECS)	1884	2000	116	Switched to USD
Netherlands East Indies Guilder (IDDG)	1828	1945	117	WWII
Italian Lira (ITL)	1882	2002	120	EURO
Peru Sol (PEH)	1864	1985	121	Hyperinflation
Spanish Peseta (ESP)	1874	2002	128	EURO
Austrian Paper Gulden (ATP)	1753	1892	139	Replaced 1:2 ATK
Belgian Franc (BEF)	1835	2002	167	EURO
Mexico Silver Peso (MXP)	1822	1992	170	Hyperinflation
Netherlands Guilder (NLG)	1814	2002	188	EURO

Source: http://dollardaze.org/blog/?page_id=0001

Appendix II – Wall Street Fines (2000-2013)

2000

| JPMorgan Chase | $ 0.2 million | 6 June |

Violations of the SEC Limit Order Display Rule and for failing to establish, maintain and enforce written supervisory procedures.

2001

| Bank of America | $ 35.6 million | 28 July |

To settle a claim that the company mismanaged its funds while acting as a trustee and paying agent for state and municipal bonds.

| JPMorgan Chase | $ 1 million | 25 September |

To settle regulators' allegations that it violated recordkeeping and reporting rules while acting as a transfer agent for bond issues.

| Bank of America | $ 22 million | 6 October |

To settle four lawsuits accusing the company of cheating thousands of personal bankers out of overtime pay.

| Goldman Sachs | $ 1 million | 27 November |

Failing to supervise an executive who was accused of conducting fraudulent trades (this fine is for Spear, Leeds & Kellogg, a unit of the Goldman Sachs Group).

2002

Wells Fargo $ 0.15 million   21 February
To settle accusations by securities regulators that
it had inadequately supervised a broker who improperly switched customers among mutual funds.

JPMorgan Chase $ 125 million   1 April
To settle a case involving more than 2 billion in
claims related to copper trades that Sumitomo said
were unauthorized.

Wells Fargo $ 42 million   17 April
To settle claims that it overcharged management
fees on trust accounts dating back to the 1970s.

Citigroup $ 215 million   19 September
Predatory lending claims.

Citigroup $ 5 million   23 September
Published misleading research.

Bank of America $ 490 million   2 October
Misrepresented financial statements.

Goldman Sachs $ 1.65 million   3 December
Violated e-mail recordkeeping requirements.

Citigroup $ 1.65 million   3 December
Violated e-mail recordkeeping requirements.

Citigroup $ 400 million   20 December
The fines were part of a settlement involving charges
that ten banks, including Chase, deceived investors
with biased research. The total settlement with the
ten banks was $ 1.4 billion. The settlement required
that the banks separate investment banking from
research, and ban any allocation of IPO shares.

2002

Goldman Sachs	$ 110 million	20 December

Fines for relief, funds for independent research and monies for investor education.

JPMorgan Chase	$ 80 million	20 December

Fines for relief, funds for independent research and monies for investor education.

2003

JPMorgan Chase	$ 6 million	20 February

Profit sharing and tie-in trades related to IPOs.

Goldman Sachs	$ 0.45 million	22 July

Settlement of accusations by the SEC that its employees helped a client to make manipulative trades (fine was for Spear, Leeds, a unit of the Goldman Sachs Group).

Citigroup	$ 101 million	28 July

Settlement concerning Enron-related allegations of misconduct.

JPMorgan Chase	$ 135 million	28 July

Settlement concerning Enron-related allegations of misconduct.

Citigroup	$ 19 million	28 July

Dealings with Dynergy.

Citigroup	$ 12.5 million	28 July

Settlement to cease and desist from further violations.

JPMorgan Chase	$ 12.5 million	28 July

Settlement to cease and desist from further violations.

2003

Goldman Sachs	$ 9.3 million	4 September

Improper trading in US Treasury Securities and futures.

JPMorgan Chase	$ 25 million	1 October

Settlement of allegations of unlawful IPO allocation practices.

Citigroup	$ 1 million	29 October

Failing to properly supervise activities.

2004

Goldman Sachs	$ 45.5 million	17 February

Alleged NYSE rule violations.

Bank of America	$ 10 million	10 March

Failing to promptly produce documents related to a regulatory investigation.

Bank of America	$ 375 million	15 March

Allegedly permitting rapid trading of certain mutual funds in its Nations Fund family.

Bank of America	$ 675 million	16 March

Illegal mutual fund trading (with FleetBoston, which was acquired by BoA).

Citigroup	$ 2.65 billion	10 May

Settlement of the WorldCom securities class action suit.

Citigroup	$ 70 million	27 May

Settlement of improper lending practices in 2000 and 2001.

2004

Goldman Sachs	$ 2 million	1 July
	Settlement of an administrative proceeding with the SEC.	
Bank of America	$ 69 million	3 July
	To settle a suit by Enron investors over the bank's role as underwriter for some debt offerings.	
Citigroup	$ 0.27 million	12 July
	Orders restitution relating to managed future sales.	
Citigroup	$ 0.25 million	19 July
	Failing to comply with their discovery obligations in 20 arbitration cases.	
Citigroup	$ 5 million	28 July
	Violations relating to recordkeeping and supervision violations.	
Goldman Sachs	$ 5 million	28 July
	Violations relating to recordkeeping and supervision violations.	
Wells Fargo	$ 6.7 million	23 August
	To settle a lawsuit that accused Wells Fargo of illegally selling customer's financial information to telemarketers.	
Citigroup, JPMorgan Chase & Bank of America	$ 111 million	1 October
	To settle a suit by the Retirement Systems of Alabama over losses stemming from the collapse of WorldCom stock and bonds.	
Citigroup	$ 0.25 million	25 October
	Disseminating inappropriate sales literature.	

2005

Goldman Sachs	$ 40 million	26 January
	Settle allegations that they sought commitments from customers to buy shares after an IPO in a move to support the price after the stock began trading.	
JPMorgan Chase	$ 2.1 Million	14 February
	Failing to keep records of all e-mail and other electronic communications and for providing incomplete records to investigators.	
Citigroup	$ 75 million	3 March
	Settlement of a lawsuit from investors over its role in the collapse of the company Global Crossing.	
Bank of America	$ 460.5 million	4 March
	Settlement with investors who bought WorldCom stock and bonds before the company filed for bankruptcy in 2002.	
JPMorgan Chase	$ 2 billion	16 March
	To settle investors' claims that it did not conduct adequate investigation into the financial condition of WorldCom before the securities were sold.	
Citigroup	$ 6.25 million	23 March
	Fined by the NASD regarding suitability and supervisory violations relating to mutual fund sales practices.	
JPMorgan Chase	$ 120 million	23 March
	To settle a shareholders lawsuit over the 1998 purchase of a Chicago bank (Bank One unit of JPMorgan Chase).	

2005

JPMorgan Chase	$ 0.15 million	9 June

Sales of restricted securities in violation of lock-up agreements as required.

Goldman Sachs	$ 0.125 million	9 June

Sales of restricted securities in violation of lock-up agreements as required.

Citigroup	$ 2 billion	10 June

Settlement of a class-action lawsuit filed by investors who argue that Citigroup helped a faltering Enron Corp. disguise billions of dollars in debt.

JPMorgan Chase	$ 2.2 billion	14 June

Agreed to pay 2.2 billion to Enron investors who accused the bank of participating in the accounting scandal that led to Enron's collapse.

Bank of America	$ 1.5 million	16 June

To settle federal regulators' charges that they violated recordkeeping rules by failing to preserve e-mail messages.

Wells Fargo	$ 34 million	11 August

To settle allegations that it imposed improper credit card processing charges.

JPMorgan Chase	$ 350 million	16 August

To settle claims over the role it played in the fraud that led to the collapse of Enron.

JPMorgan Chase	$ 0.1 million	20 September

Failing to file official statements from municipal bond offerings.

Wells Fargo	$ 3 million	19 December

For suitability and supervisory violations.

2006

JPMorgan Chase	$ 425 million	20 April

To settle its part of a class-action lawsuit that contends that dozen of banks cheated investors out of hundreds of million of dollars from IPOs during the 1990s market boom.

Goldman Sachs, Citigroup, Bear Stearns, Lehman Brothers, Merrill Lynch, JPMorgan Chase and Morgan Stanley	$ 13 million in total	1 June

Settlement of claims that they favoured some customers in the $ 200 billion market for auction-rate bonds.

Citigroup	$ 0.775 million	17 July

Fined for deficient price target, ratings and other disclosures in research reports.

Citigroup	$ 1.1 million	10 August

Fined for failing to prevent brokers' submission of false information.

Bank of America	$ 7.5 million	27 September

Settlement of a money laundering suit.

Wells Fargo	$ 12.8 million	6 October

To settle a class-action lawsuit that claimed some workers were improperly exempted from overtime pay.

Citigroup	$ 0.85 million	16 October

Fined by the NASD for supervisory, recordkeeping, telemarketing and other violations.

JPMorgan Chase	$ 2.2 million	22 November

To settle claims that the company's Bank One unit discriminated against hundreds of employees on long-term medical leave.

2006

Citigroup, Bank of America, JPMorgan Chase, Wachovia and 35 other banks	$ 255 million in total	9 December
	Settle a lawsuit with the investors in Adelphia Communications, the bankrupt cable television company. The amount each bank owed was confidential.	
Citigroup, JPMorgan Chase and other defendants	$ 4.5 million	28 December
	To settle any liability related to the fraud that destroyed Enron five years ago.	

2007

Bank of America	$ 0.55 million	16 January
	Fined by the NYSE Regulation because of the violation of the so-called 'firm quote' rule.	
Goldman Sachs	$ 0.6 million	16 January
	Fined by the NYSE Regulation because of the violation of the so-called 'firm quote' rule.	
Bank of America	$ 3 million	29 January
	Failing to comply with anti-money laundering rules in connection with high-risk accounts.	
Goldman Sachs	$ 2 million	14 March
	To settle 'naked' short-selling case.	
Bank of America	$ 26 Million	15 March
	To settle charges that its securities published fraudulent research reports on companies and failed to prevent leaks of reports that were used for improper trading.	
Wells Fargo	$ 6.8 million	26 April
	Settle a class-action lawsuit accusing it of improper nonprime mortgage lending practices.	

2007

Citigroup	$ 15 million	6 June

Fined by the NASD to settle charges related to misleading documents and inadequate disclosure in retirement seminars and meetings for BellSouth Corp.

Wells Fargo	$ 0.25 million	28 June

For failing to disclose in a research report that an analyst had taken a job with the company she was recommending.

JPMorgan Chase	$ 0.5 million	13 December

Failing to disclose payments to consultants to obtain numerous municipal securities offerings.

2008

Goldman Sachs	$ 11.5 million	5 February

Settlement in Enron securities lawsuit.

Citigroup	$ 1.66 billion	25 March

Agreed to pay 1.66 billion to creditors of Enron who lost money when the energy trader collapsed in 2001.

Citigroup	$ 33 million	4 April

To settle a gender-discrimination lawsuit.

Citigroup	$ 100 million	8 August

To settle claims that the bank misled investors to buy auction-rate securities.

JPMorgan Chase	$ 25 million	14 August

To settle claims that the bank misled investors to buy auction-rate securities.

2008

Goldman Sachs	$ 22.5 million	21 August

Settlement with state regulators for telling investors that auction-rate debt was as safe and liquid as cash.

Citigroup	$ 18 million	26 August

Settlement of accusations that it wrongly took funds from accounts of credit card customers.

Citigroup	$ 0.3 million	13 December

Failing to supervise commissions charged to customers on stock and option trades.

2009

Goldman Sachs	$ 5 million	4 March

Settlement of SEC's charges that it systematically cheated their costumers of millions of dollars by improperly slicing bits of profit from countless trades.

Citigroup	$ 2 Million	17 March

Fined for range of trade reporting violations.

JPMorgan Chase, Goldman Sachs, Morgan Stanley, Credit Suisse, Bear Stearns, Lehman Brothers, AIG and others.	586 million in total	1 April

To resolve litigation over claims of fraud in the pricing of IPOs in the late 1990s.

Citigroup	$ 1.72 million	15 April

To settle allegations that it misled clients into thinking that the auction-rate securities they were buying were liquid like cash.

2009

Goldman Sachs	$ 60 million	11 June
	Settlement as part of a state investigation into subprime lending.	
Wells Fargo	$ 40 million	9 July
	To settle claims that employees misled investors about the value and safety of certain securities during the financial crisis.	
Bank of America	$ 33 million	3 August
	Misleading investors about billions of dollars in bonuses that were paid to Merrill Lynch executives at the time of the acquisition of the firm.	
Citigroup	$ 0.425 million	22 September
	Supervisory failures in Vonage IPO.	
JPMorgan Chase, Bear Stearns, Morgan Stanley and Credit Suisse Group	$ 100 million in total	10 October
	To settle a lawsuit over their roles in the bankruptcy of a Philadelphia mortgage lender.	
Citigroup	$ 0.6 million	12 October
	Failing to supervise tax-related stock transactions.	
JPMorgan Chase	$ 0.664 million	24 October
	To settle allegations that it misled clients into thinking that the auction-rate securities they were buying were liquid like cash.	
JPMorgan Chase	$ 75 million	3 November
	Company had made unlawful payments to friends of Jefferson County's commissioners in a scheme to win lucrative business from the county to sell bonds and trade in derivatives.	

2009

Wells Fargo	$ 1.9 million	18 November

Misleading clients by falsely assuring them
that auction rate securities were a safe, liquid
alternative to cash, certificates of deposit or money
market funds.

2010

Wells Fargo	$ 160 million	17 March

Wachovia Bank, a unit of Wells Fargo, has agreed to
pay to settle accusations that it laundered Mexican
drug money.

Citigroup	$ 0.65 million	6 April

Fined for direct borrow program deficiencies.

Citigroup	$ 1.5 million	26 May

Supervisory failures related to elaborate scheme to
misappropriate millions in trust funds belonging
to cemeteries.

JPMorgan Chase	$ 48.6 million	3 June

Fined by the financial regulator in the UK for failing
to keep client funds separate from the firm's money.

Goldman Sachs	$ 550 million	15 July

Settlement with the SEC concerning materi-
ally misstated and omitted facts in disclosure
documents for a synthetic CDO product (Abacus
2007-AC1).

Citigroup	$ 75 million	29 July

Settlement of civil charges that it had misled
investors over potential losses from high-risk
mortgages.

2010

Bank of America — $ 108 million — 2 August
Countrywide Financial, acquired by Bank of America, agreed to pay 108 million to settle federal charges that the company overcharged customers who were struggling to hang onto their homes.

Bank of America — $ 600 million — 3 August
Countrywide Financial, acquired by Bank of America, agreed to pay 600 million to settle shareholder lawsuits in the largest payout so far from the mortgage crisis.

Wells Fargo — $ 203 million — 9 August
The bank manipulated debit-card transactions without their knowledge to increase revenue from overdraft fees.

Bank of America — $ 150 million — 1 September
Settlement between the SEC and BoA related to the acquisition of Merrill Lynch.

Goldman Sachs — $ 27 million — 8 September
Fined by the British securities regulator for not disclosing the SEC's inquiry into the synthetic CDO (Abacus).

Bank of America, Citigroup, JPMorgan Chase, Wells Fargo and more than 20 other banks — $ 175 million — 22 October
To settle a suit with legal trust pursuing claims on behalf of bankrupt Adelphia Communications Corp.

Goldman Sachs — $ 0.65 million — 9 September
Failing to disclose Wells notices.

2010

Wells Fargo $ 100 million 20 November
Paid to Citigroup to resolve claims that it had
unfairly wrestled Wachovia out of Citi's hands.

Bank of America $ 137 million 7 December
To settle charges from the SEC and state and federal
authorities related to its participation in a bid-
rigging scheme in the municipal securities markets
as a part of a continuing federal investigation.

2011

Bank of America $ 410 million 23 May
To settle its piece of a broad lawsuit involving
excessive overdraft fees on debit cards.

Bank of America $ 20 million 26 May
Settlement of federal complaints that they
(Countrywide Financial) wrongfully foreclosed on
the homes of military service members (most of
the foreclosures began before Bank of America
acquired Countrywide).

Wells Fargo $ 11.2 million 4 April
Selling certain mortgage-backed securities while
they knew they were worth far less than face value.

Goldman Sachs $ 10 million 9 June
Agreed to pay a $ 10 million fine and stop holding
private meetings of stock analysts and traders
known as 'huddles' to settle an investigation by
Massachusetts's chief securities regulator.

2011

JPMorgan Chase	$ 153.6 million	20 June

To settle federal civil accusations that it misled investors in a complex mortgage securities transaction in 2007, just as the housing market was beginning to plummet.

Bank of America	$ 8.5 billion	28 June

To settle claims from investors about purchased mortgage securities.

JPMorgan Chase	$ 211 million	6 July

To resolve allegations that it cheated governments in 31 states by rigging the bidding process for reinvesting the proceeds of dozens of municipal bonds.

Wells Fargo	$ 125 Million	7 July

To settle a lawsuit over the sale of mortgage pass-through certificates.

Wells Fargo	$ 85 million	20 July

To settle civil charges that it falsified loan documents and pushed borrowers toward subprime mortgages with higher interest rates during the housing boom.

Wells Fargo	$ 590 million	5 August

To settle accusations that Wachovia, acquired by Wells Fargo, made misleading disclosures relating to the sale of securities between 2006 and 2008.

Citigroup	$ 0.5 million	9 August

Failing to supervise a sales assistant who misappropriated customer funds.

JPMorgan Chase	$ 88.3 million	24 August

Settlement with the Treasury Department over a series of transactions involving Cuba, Iran and Sudan.

Citigroup	$ 0.77 million	3 October

Hong Kong's regulator has fined Citigroup for failing to report a Ponzi scheme involving one of its former employees.

Citigroup	$ 285 million	18 October

Settlement of the SEC's charges that it defrauded investors who bought toxic housing-related debt that the bank believed would fail.

Wells Fargo	$ 37 million	7 November

Accused of rigging the bidding competition for business from state and local governments.

Wells Fargo	$ 0.3 million	22 November

Use of misleading marketing materials for REIT offering.

Wells Fargo	$ 75 million	2 December

To settle a class-action lawsuit brought by stockholders who claimed Wachovia misrepresented the quality of its mortgages from 2006 to 2008.

Bank of America	$ 315 million	6 December

To settle claims by investors that they were misled about mortgage-backed investments sold by its Merrill Lynch unit.

2011

Wells Fargo	$ 148 million	7 December

Settlement of charges that Wachovia Bank, now part of Wells Fargo, reaped millions of dollars in profits by rigging bids in the municipal securities market.

Goldman Sachs	$ 10 million	14 December

To settle claims over its handling of hedge-fund trading in the Arthur Nadel Ponzi Scheme.

Wells Fargo	$ 2 million	15 December

Unsuitable sales of reverse convertibles to elderly customers and failure to provide breakpoints on UIT sales.

Bank of America	$ 335 million	20 December

To settle allegations that its Countrywide Financial unit discriminated against black and Hispanic borrowers during the housing boom.

2012

Goldman Sachs	$ 1 Million	11 January

To settle a suit brought by a group of computer technicians who said they weren't paid overtime for their work as contractors.

Citigroup	$ 0.725 Million	18 January

Fined for failure to disclose conflicts of interest in research reports and public appearances by research analysts.

Wells Fargo	$ 75 Million	27 January

Settlement of class-action lawsuit against Wachovia, acquired by Wells Fargo, over mortgage loans.

JPMorgan Chase	$ 110 Million	6 February

To settle consumer litigation accusing it of
charging excessive overdraft fees.

Citigroup, Bank of America, Wells Fargo, JPMorgan Chase & Ally Financial (the old GMAC).	$ 25 Billion	6 February

Settlement with the government to end a
nationwide investigation of abusive foreclosure
practices stemming from the collapse of the
housing bubble.

Bank of America	$ 164 Million	9 February

Settlement with the Office of the Comptroller
of the Currency (OCC) on civil money penalties
in connection with the unsafe and unsound
mortgage servicing and foreclosure practices that
were subject to comprehensive cease and desist
orders issued by the OCC in April 2011.

JPMorgan Chase	$ 113 Million	9 February

Settlement with the OCC on civil money penalties
in connection with the unsafe and unsound
mortgage servicing and foreclosure practices that
were subject to comprehensive cease and desist
orders issued by the OCC in April 2011.

Wells Fargo	$ 83 Million	9 February

Settlement with the OCC on civil money penalties
in connection with the unsafe and unsound
mortgage servicing and foreclosure practices that
were subject to comprehensive cease and desist
orders issued by the OCC in April 2011.

2012

Citigroup $ 34 Million   9 February
Settlement with the OCC on civil money penalties
in connection with the unsafe and unsound
mortgage servicing and foreclosure practices that
were subject to comprehensive cease and desist
orders issued by the OCC in April 2011.

Citigroup $ 158 Million   15 February
To settle US civil claims that it defrauded the
government into insuring thousands of risky home
loans by its CitiMortgage unit.

JPMorgan Chase $ 45 Million   13 March
To settle a lawsuit alleging it charged veterans
hidden fees in mortgage refinancing.

Goldman Sachs $ 7 Million   13 March
Settlement with the CFTC over charges that it
failed to diligently supervise activity in trading
accounts.

Citigroup $ 1.248 Million   19 March
Fined for charging excessive markups and
markdowns on corporate and agency bond
transactions and for related supervisory violations.
Note: the fine was 0.6 million; the remaining
$ 0.648 million was paid as restitutions to clients.

JPMorgan Chase $ 20 Million   4 April
Civil monetary penalty to settle CFTC charges of
unlawfully handling customer segregated funds.

| Goldman Sachs | $ 22 Million | 12 April |

Fined by the SEC for failing to supervise equity research analysts' communications with traders and clients and for failing to adequately monitor trading in advance of published research changes to detect and prevent possible information breaches by its research analysts.

| Wells Fargo | $ 2.741 Million | 1 May |

Fined for selling leveraged and inverse ETFs without reasonable supervision and for not having a reasonable basis for recommending the securities. Note: the fine was $ 2.1 million; the remaining 0.641 million was paid as restitutions to clients.

| Citigroup | $ 2.146 Million | 1 May |

Fined for selling leveraged and inverse ETFs without reasonable supervision and for not having a reasonable basis for recommending the securities. Note: the fine was $ 2 million the remaining $ 0.146 million was paid as restitutions to clients.

| Citigroup | $ 3.5 Million | 22 May |

Fined for providing inaccurate performance data related to subprime securitizations.

| Bank of America | $ 2.8 Million | 21 June |

Bank of America's Merrill Lynch wealth-management unit was fined for overbilling customers over an eight-year period.

| Goldman Sachs | $ 30 Million | 28 June |

Settlement of a legal dispute that originated from a multimillion-dollar breach of contract and fraud lawsuit.

2012

Wells Fargo 175 Million 12 July
To settle accusations that its independent brokers discriminated against black and Hispanic borrowers during the housing boom.

Bank of America $ 375 Million 17 July
To settle a case brought by Syncora Guarantee over toxic mortgage-backed securities during the 2008 crisis. Syncora said it was duped into insuring the mortgage-backed securities and that the quality of the underlying mortgages was misrepresented.

JPMorgan Chase $ 100 Million 24 July
To settle litigation by credit card customers who accused the bank of improperly boosting their minimum payments as a means to generate higher fees.

Goldman Sachs $ 26 Million 31 July
To settle a lawsuit brought by investors in a mortgage-backed securities offering, where the bank did not conduct proper due diligence.

Wells Fargo $ 6.58 Million 14 August
To settle civil charges alleging it sold complex mortgage-backed instruments to municipalities and non-profits during the financial crisis without fully disclosing the risks.

Citigroup $ 590 Million 29 August
To settle a shareholder lawsuit accusing the bank of failing to disclose fully its exposure to toxic mortgage products in the run-up to the financial crisis.

Citigroup $ 0.525 Million   21 September
                         Fined by the CFTC for exceeding speculative
                         position limits in wheat futures contracts.

Goldman Sachs $ 12 Million   27 September
                         To settle charges that one of its former bankers
                         worked on the campaign of a politician in Mas-
                         sachusetts in the US while trying to win business
                         from the state.

JPMorgan Chase $ 0.6 Million   27 September
                         Penalty for violating cotton futures speculative
                         position limits.

Bank of America $ 2.43 Billion   28 September
                         To settle a class-action lawsuit related to its acquisi-
                         tion of Merrill Lynch at the height of the financial
                         crisis. The bank was accused of providing false and
                         misleading statements about the health of the firm,
                         which, unknown to the public, was racking up huge
                         losses in late 2008 amid turmoil in the markets.

Goldman Sachs $ 6.75 Million   8 October
                         To settle allegations it improperly marked trading
                         orders that may have allowed some traders to
                         execute their orders ahead of others.

Citigroup $ 2 Million   26 October
                         Fined for leaking confidential information
                         about Facebook IPO to a popular tech blog. The
                         employee who did this was fired.

JPMorgan Chase $ 417 Million   16 November
                         Settlement with the SEC over packaging and sale
                         of troubled mortgage securities to investors.

2012

Goldman Sachs

$ 1.5 Million   7 December

To settle charges it failed to supervise its traders and that it allowed one futures dealer to hide billions in dollars from sight and causing a $ 118 million loss.

Citigroup

$ 1.279 Million   27 December

Fined for unfairly obtaining the reimbursement of fees they paid to the California Public Securities Association from the proceeds of municipal and state bond offerings. Note: the fine was 0.888 million; the remaining 0.391 million was paid out as restitutions to clients.

Goldman Sachs

$ 0.684 Million   27 December

Fined for unfairly obtaining the reimbursement of fees they paid to the California Public Securities Association from the proceeds of municipal and state bond offerings. Note: the fine was 0.568 million; the remaining 0.116 million was paid out as restitutions to clients.

JPMorgan Chase

$ 0.632 Million   27 December

Fined for unfairly obtaining the reimbursement of fees they paid to the California Public Securities Association from the proceeds of municipal and state bond offerings. Note: the fine was 0.465 million; the remaining 0.167 million was paid out as restitutions to clients.

2013

Bank of America $ 10.3 Billion 7 January

Settlement with Fannie Mae to deal with questionable home loans it sold to the government-backed mortgage financer during the housing bubble. The bank will pay 3.55 billion in cash to Fannie Mae and it will also purchase 30,000 questionable mortgages for 6.75 billion that are likely to produce losses.

Bank of America $ 2.9 Billion 7 January

Settlement for deficient practices on mortgage servicing and processing, improper fees, wrongful denial of modification and the robo-signing scandal (the practice of assigning bank employees to rapidly approve numerous foreclosures with only cursory glances at the glut of paperwork to determine if all the documents are in order).

Wells Fargo $ 1.97 Billion 7 January

Settlement for deficient practices on mortgage servicing and processing, improper fees, wrongful denial of modification and the robo-signing scandal.

JPMorgan Chase $ 1.95 Billion 7 January

Settlement for deficient practices on mortgage servicing and processing, improper fees, wrongful denial of modification and the robo-signing scandal.

Citigroup $ 794 Million 7 January

Settlement for deficient practices on mortgage servicing and processing, improper fees, wrongful denial of modification and the robo-signing scandal.

Goldman Sachs	$ 330 Million	7 January

Settlement for deficient practices on mortgage servicing and processing, improper fees, wrongful denial of modification and the robo-signing scandal.

Goldman Sachs	$ 330 Million	16 January

To settle a federal probe into allegations that the bank improperly seized homes.

Citigroup	$ 730 Million	19 March

To settle claims that it misled debt investors about its condition during the financial crisis.

JPMorgan Chase	$ 546 Million	20 March

Settlement in the MF Global dispute.

Bank of America	$ 1 Million	16 April

Fined Bank of America's Merrill Lynch in a civil action for not getting the best execution price customer transaction involving non-convertible preferred securities and failing to properly supervise the process.

Bank of America	$ 500 Million	17 April

Settlement with investors who claimed they were misled by its Countrywide unit into buying risky mortgage debt.

JPMorgan Chase	$ 4.5 Million	23 May

Fined by the UK markets regulator for failing to keep up-to-date records of clients and lacking risk and compliance controls.

Citigroup	Unknown	28 May

Settlement with a federal agency that had accused the bank of misleading Fannie Mae and Freddie Mac into buying $ 3.5 billion of mortgage-backed securitises. Settlement was 'satisfactory' according to the FHFA, but declined to say how much the bank would pay.

Bank of America	$ 0.9 Million	4 June

Fined for losses incurred from unsuitable sales of floating-rate bank loan funds.

Wells Fargo	$ 1.25 Million	4 June

Fined for losses incurred from unsuitable sales of floating-rate bank loan funds.

Citigroup	$ 968 Million	1 July

To settle claims that Citi sold faulty mortgages to Fannie Mae.

JPMorgan Chase	$ 410 Million	30 July

To settle US Federal Energy Regulatory Commission allegations that the bank manipulated power markets and enriched itself at the expense of consumers.

JPMorgan Chase	$ 23 Million	16 August

To settle a lawsuit accusing it of mishandling money of pension funds and other clients by investing it in notes from Lehman Brothers, which later went bankrupt.

Bank of America	$ 160 Million	28 August

Bank of America's Merrill Lynch settled a class-action race discrimination lawsuit.

2013

Bank of America $ 39 Million 8 September
To settle claims of gender bias by women in its
Merrill Lynch brokerage division.

JPMorgan Chase 300 Million 9 September
Settlement to resolve accusations that they forced
homeowners into overpriced property insurance
and entered into kickback arrangements that
inflated the policies' prices.

Wells Fargo $ 869 Million 1 October
To resolve disputes over faulty loans sold to the
government-backed firm before 1 January 2009.

JPMorgan Chase $ 920 Million 20 September
JPMorgan Chase, settling US and UK probes of a
$ 6.2 billion trading loss, agreed to pay 920 million
in penalties and admitted violating securities laws
last year as top managers withheld information
from the board.

Citibank $ 395 Million 25 September
Agreed to pay $ 395 million to Freddie Mac as part
of a settlement over defective mortgages sold to
the government-controlled home-loan financier,
the bank said Wednesday.

JPMorgan Chase $ 13 Billion 26 October
To settle Federal Housing Finance Agency claims
related to home loans and mortgage-backed
securities the company sold to Fannie Mae and
Freddie Mac. And misleading investors over
bundling subprime mortgages into bonds before
the financial crisis.

The total amount of fines and settlements paid by Wall Street Banks between 2000 and 2013, to avoid prosecution, adds up to almost $ 100 billion.

* US housing regulators are looking to fine Bank of America more than $ 6 billion for its role in misleading mortgage agencies during the housing boom, compared with the $ 4 billion to be paid by JPMorgan Chase & Co.[279]

When we add this extra settlement, the total amount paid rises to over $ 100 billion.

List of all financial settlements with Wall Street Banks since 2000.

Amount of Fines (in USD millions)

year	BoA	Citi	JPM	GS	WF	Other	Total bln $
2000	0	0	0	0	0	0	0
2001	58	0	1	1	0	0	60
2002	490	620	205	112	42	0	1.469
2003	0	134	179	10	0	0	322
2004	1.100	2.7	0	53	7	111	4.027
2005	462	2.100	4.700	40	37	0	7.293
2006	8	3	427	0	13	243	693
2007	30	15	1	3	7	0	55
2008	0	1.800	25	34	0	0	1.870
2009	33	4	76	65	42	686	906
2010	995	77	49	578	463	175	2.300
2011	9.300	286	453	20	1.400	0	11.400
2012	2.900	793	806	107	342	25.000	30.000
2013*	13.900	2.900	17.200	330	2.8	0	37.100
Totals:	29.300	11.400	24.000	1.400	5.900	26.200	97.600

Source: The Big Reset research

279 http://www.reuters.com/article/2013/10/20/us-bofa-settlement-idUSBRE-99J0AW20131020

Bibliography

Ahamed, Liaquat, *Lords of finance: The bankers who broke the world*. The Penguin Press, 2009.

Allen, Gary, *None Dare Call it Conspiracy*. Concord Press, 1972.

Angell, Marcia M.D., *The Truth About the Drug Companies: How They Deceive Us and What To Do About It*. Random House, 2005.

Baker, James C., *The Bank for International Settlements: Evolution and Evaluation*. Quorum Books, 2002.

Bartlett, Bruce, *Impostor: How George W. Bush Bankrupted America and Betrayed the Reagan Legacy*. Doubleday, 2006.

Batra, Ravi, *De Grote Wereldcrisis van 1990*. Omega Boek, 1988.

Batra, Ravi, *Greenspan's Fraud: How Two Decades of His Policies Have Undermined the Global Economy*. Palgrave MacMillan, 2005.

Batra, Ravi, *The Crash of the Millennium: Surviving the Coming Inflationary Depression*. Harmony Books, 1999.

Ben-Menasche, Ari, *Profits of War: Inside the Secret US-Israeli Arms Network*. Sheridan Square Press, 1992.

Bernstein, Peter L., *Against the Gods: The Remarkable Story of Risk*. John Wiley & Sons, 1998.

Bernstein, Peter L., *The Power of Gold: The History of an Obsession*. John Wiley & Sons, 2000.

Blackburn, Simon, *Politeia van Plato*. Mets & Schilt, 2008.

Bonner, Bill & Adison Wiggin, *Empire of Debt*. John Wiley & Sons, 2006.

Bonner, Bill & Adison Wiggin, *Financial Reckoning Day: Surviving the Soft Depression of the 21st Century*. John Wiley & Sons, 2003.

Brenner, Reuven & Gabrielle A. Brenner, *Gambling and Speculation: A Theory, a History, and a Future of Some Human Decisions*. Cambridge University Press, 1990.

Bresciani-Turroni, Costantino, *The Economics of Inflation*. M. Kelley Publishers, 1931.

Brzezinski, Zbigniew, *The Grand Chessboard: American Primacy and its Geostrategic Imperatives*. Basic Books, 1997.

Carmack, Patrick S. J., *The Money Masters*. Still Productions, 1996.

Carlin, Peter & James Sinclair, *A Pocketbook of Gold*. P. Carlin, 2010.

Chancellor, Edward, *Devil Take the Hindmost: A History of Financial Speculation*. Plume, 2000.

Chernow, Ron, *The House of Morgan: An American Banking Dynasty and the Rise of Modern Finance*. Simon & Schuster, 1990.

Colbert, David, *Eyewitness to Wall Street: Four Hundred Years of Dreamers, Schemers, Buts and Booms*. Broadway Books, 2001.

Coleman, John, *Conspirator's Hierarchy: The Story of the Committee of 300*. America West Publishers, 1992.

Coleman, John, *Diplomacy by Deception*. Bridger House Publishers, 1993.

Coleman, John, *One World Order, Socialist Dictatorship*. Bridger House Publishers, 1998.

Coombs, Charles A., *The Arena of International Finance*. Wiley & Sons, 1976.

Cramer, James J., *Confessions of a Street Addict*. Simon & Schuster, 2002.

Dall, Curtis B., *F.D.R.: My Exploited Father-In-Law*. Christian Crusade Publications, 1967.

Davidson, James Dale & Lord William Rees-Mogg, *The Great Reckoning: Protect Yourself in the Coming Depression*. Touchstone, 1993.

Davies, G., *A History of Money: From Ancient Times to the Present Day*. University of Wales Press, 1994.

De Grand Pre, Donn, *The Viper's Venom*. Grand Pre Books, 2002.

Duncan, Richard, *The Dollar Crisis*. John Wiley & Sons, 2005.

Ebeling, Richard M., *The Austrian Theory of the Trade Cycle, and other essays*. Mises Institute, 1996.

Engdahl, William, *A Century of War: Anglo-American Oil Politics and the New World Order*. Pluto Press, 2004.

Engdahl, William, *God of Money: Wall Street and the Death of the American Century*. Edition Engdahl, 2009.

Epperson, A. Ralph, *The New World Order*. Publius Press, 2005.

Faber, Marc, *Tomorrow's Gold: Asia's Age of Discovery*. CLSA Books, 2002.

Fentrop, Paul, *Ondernemingen en hun aandeelhouders sinds de VOC*. Prometheus, 2002.

Ferguson, Niall, *The Ascent of Money*. The Penguin Press, 2008.

Fraser, Steve, *Wall Street: A Cultural History*. Faber and Faber, 2005.

Friedman, Milton & Anna J. Schwartz, *A Monetary History of the United States, 1867-1960*. Princeton University Press, 1971.

Fukuyama, Francis, *Trust*. Free Press Paperbacks, 1995.

Galbraith, John Kenneth, *A Short History of Financial Euphoria*. Penguin Books, 1994.

Galbraith, John Kenneth, *The Great Crash, 1929*. Houghton Mifflin Company, 1997.

Gavin, Francis J., Gold, *Dollars & Power*. The University of North Carolina Press, 2004.

Gelsi, Steve, *How America Made a Fortune and Lost Its Shirt*. Alpha, 2002.

Gertz, Bill, *The China Threat: How the People's Republic Targets America*. Regnery Publishing, 2000.

Gough, Leo, *Asia Meltdown: The End of the Miracle?* Capstone Publishing Limited, 1998.

Grant, James, *The Trouble with Prosperity: A Contrarian's Tale of Boom, Bust and Speculation*. Times Business, 1996.

Greider, William, *The Secrets of the Temple: How the Federal Reserve Runs the Country*. Touchstone Books, 1987.

Griffin, Edward G., *The Creature from Jekyll Island: A Second Look at the Federal Reserve*. American Media, 2002.

Hayes, Declan, *Japan's Big Bang: The Deregulation and Revitalization of the Japanese Economy*. Tuttle Publishing, 2000

Hourani, Albert, *A History of the Arab Peoples*. Faber and Faber, 2005.

Hudson, Michael, *Super Imperialism: The Origins and Fundamentals of US World Dominance*. Pluto Press, 2003.

Hulbert, Mark, *The Untold Story of American banks, Oil Interests, The Shah's Money, Debts and the Astounding Connections Between Them*. Richardson & Snyder, 1982.

Huntington, Samuel P., *The Clash of Civilizations and the Remaking of World Order*. Touchstone Books, 1998.

Jensen, Derrick, *Endgame*. Seven Stories Press, 2006.

Johnson, Chalmers, *The Sorrows of Empire*. Henry Holt and Company, 2004.

Jones, Alan B., *How the World Really Works*. ABJ Press, 1996.

Kagan, Robert & William Kristol, *Present Dangers. Crisis and Opportunity in American Foreign and Defense Policy*. Encounter Books, 2000.

Kelley, Kitty, *The Family: The Real Story of the Bush Dynasty*. Doubleday, 2004.

Kennedy, Paul, *Preparing for the Twenty-First Century*. Vintage Books, 1994.

Kennedy, Paul, *The Rise and Fall of the Great Powers*. Vintage Books, 1989.

Kindleberger, Charles P., Manias, *Panics and Crashes: A History of Financial Crises*. John Wiley & Sons, 1996.

Kindleberger, Charles P., *The World in Depression, 1929-1939*. University of California Press, 1986.

Klare, Michael T., *Blood and Oil: The Dangers and Consequences of America's Growing Dependency on Imported Oil*. Henry Holt and Company, 2004.

Kotlikoff, Laurence J. & Scott Burns, *The Coming Generational Storm: What You Need to Know about America's Future*. The MIT Press, 2004.

Krugman, Paul, *The Return of Depression Economics*. W.W. Norton & Company, 1999.

Kurzwell, Ray, *The Singularity is Near*. Viking Penguin, 2005.

Leeb, Stephen, *The Oil Factor*. Warner Business Books, 2004.

Lefèvre, Edwin, *Reminiscences of a Stock Operator*. John Wiley & Sons, 1994.

Leggett, Jeremy, T*he Empty Tank: Oil, Gas, Hot Air and the Coming Global Financial Catastrophe*. Random House, 2005.

Levitt, Arthur & Paula Dwyer, *Take on the Street: What Wall Street and Corporate America Don't Want You to Know*. Pantheon Books, 2002.

Lewis, Michael, *Boomerang: Travels in the New Third World*. W.W. Norton & Company, 2011.

Lietaer, Bernard A., *Mysterium Geld: Emotionale Bedeutung und Wirkungsweise eines Tabus*. Riemann Verlag, 2000.

Lips, Ferdinand, *Gold Wars: The Battle Against Sound Money as Seen From a Swiss Perspective*. FAME (Foundation for the Advancement of Monetary Education), 2002.

Lorenz, Chris, *If you're so smart, why aren't you rich?* Universiteit markt & management. Uitgeverij Boom, 2008.

Lowenstein, Roger, *When Genius Failed: The Rise and Fall of Long-Term Capital Management*. Random House, 2000.

Lynch, Peter & John Rothschild, *One Up on Wall Street: How to Use What You Already Know to Make Money in the Market*. Fireside, 2000.

Mackay, Charles & Joseph de la Vega, *Extraordinary Popular Delusions and the Madness of Crowds*. John Wiley & Sons, 1996.

Maier, Nicholas W., *Trading With the Enemy: Seduction and Betrayal on Jim Cramer's Wall Street*. Harper Business, 2002.

Mallaby, Sebastian, *More money than God*. The Penguin Press, 2010.

Maloney, Michael, *Guide to Investing in Gold & Silver*. Business Plus, 2008.

Mauldin, John, *Bull's Eye Investing: Targeting Real Returns in a Smoke and Mirrors Market*. John Wiley & Sons, 2004.

Mauldin, John & Jonathan Tepper, *Endgame*. John Wiley & Sons, 2010.

Martenson, Chris, *The Crash Course*. John Wiley & Sons, 2011.

McDonough, William & Michael Braungart, *Cradle to Cradle: Remaking the Way We Make Things*. North Point Press, 2002.

McFadden, Louis T., *Collective speeches of Congressman Louis T. McFadden.* Omni Publications, 1970.

McKillop, Andrew, et al., *The Final Energy Crisis*. Pluto Press, 2005.

Mecking, Eric, *Deflatie in aantocht: De historische achtergronden van de krediet-crisis en de komende grote depressie*. Mets & Schilt, 2005/2008.

Meltzer, Allan H., *A History of the Federal Reserve*, Volume 2, Book 2, 1970-1986. University of Chicago Press, 2010.

Middelkoop, Willem, *Als de dollar valt: Wat bankiers en politici u niet vertellen over geld en de kredietcrisis*. Nieuw Amsterdam, 2007.

Middelkoop, Willem, *Overleef de kredietcrisis*. Nieuw Amsterdam, 2009.

Mishkin, Frederic S., *The Economics of Money, Banking and Financial Markets*, Pearson Education Limited, 2006.

Morley, John, *The Life Of William Ewart Gladstone*, Cambridge University Press, 1903.

Morris, Charles R., *The Trillion Dollar Meltdown: Easy Money, High Rollers and the Great Credit Crash*. Public Affairs, 2008.

Mullins, Eustace, *The Secrets of the Federal Reserve*. Red Planet Books, 1993.

Naisbitt, John & Patricia Aburdene, *Megatrends 2000*. Pan Books, 1990.

Noble, Thomas F. X., Barry Strauss, Duane J. Osheim, Kristen B. Neuschel, Elinor A. Accampo, David D. Roberts en William B. Cohen, *Western Civilization Beyond Bounderies*. Wadsworth, 2008.

Orlov, Dmitry, *Reinventing collapse*. New Society Publishers, 2011.

Otte, Max, *Der Crash kommt: Die neue Weltwirtschaftskrise und wie Sie sich darauf vorbereiten*, Ullstein, 2008.

Palast, Greg, *The Best Democracy Money Can Buy: The Truth about Corporate Cons, Globalization and High-Finance Fraudsters*. Penguin Books, 2003.

Partnoy, Frank, *Infectious Greed: How Deceit and Risk Corrupted the Financial Markets*. Profile Books, 2003.

Partnoy, Frank, *Fiasco: The Inside Story of a Wall Street Trader*. Penguin Books, 1999.

Paul, Ron, *End the Fed*. Grand Central Publishing, 2009.

Perkins, John, *Confessions of an Economic Hitman*. Berret-Koehler Publishers, 2004.

Perloff, James, *The Shadows of Power: The Council on Foreign Relations and the American Decline*. Western Islands, 2005.

Peterson, Peter G., *Running on Empty*. Farrar, Straus and Giroux, 2004.

Pick, Franz, *1975-1976 Pick's Currency Yearbook*. Pick Pub. Corp., 1975.

Polo, Marco, *Il Milione*, Polak & van Gennep, 2001.

Prechter, Robert R., *At the Crest of the Tidal Wave: A Forecast for the Great Bear Market*. John Wiley & Sons, 2001.

Prechter, Robert R. *Conquer the Crash: You Can Survive and Prosper in a Deflationary Depression*. John Wiley & Sons, 2009.

Quigley, Caroll, *The Anglo-American Establishment*. GSG & Associates, 1981.

Quigley, Caroll, *Tragedy and Hope: A History of the World in Our Time*. Macmillan, 1966.

Rand, Ayn, *Atlas in staking*. Uitgeverij Boekenmaker, 2007.

Rand, Ayn, *Capitalism: The Unknown Ideal*. Signet, 1967.

Reinhart, Carmen M. and Kenneth Rogoff, *This Time is Different: Eight Centuries of Financial Folly*. Princeton University Press, 2009

Rickards, James, *Currency Wars: The Making of the Next Global Crisis*. Penguin Group Inc, 2011.

Rifkin, Jeremy, *The Age of Access: The New Culture of Hypercapitalism, Where All of Life is a Paid-for Experience*. Tarcher/Putnam Books, 2000.

Roberts, Paul, *The End of Oil: On the Edge of a Perilous New World*. First Mariner Books, 2005.

Rogers, Jim, *Adventure Capitalist*. Random House, 2003.

Rogers, Jim, *Hot Commodities*. Random House, 2004.

Rosoff, Stephen M., Henry N. Pontell & Robert H. Tillman, *Looting America: Greed, Corruption, Villains and Victims*. Pearson Education, 2003.

Rothbard, Murray N., *The Case Against the Fed*. Ludwig von Mises Institute, 1994.

Rothbard, Murray N., *The Mysteries of Banking*. Richardson & Snyder, 1983.

Rothchild, John, *The Bear Book: Survive and Profit in Ferocious Markets*. John Wiley & Sons, 1998.

Rueff, Jacques, *The Monetary Sin of the West*. The Macmillan Company, 1972.

Ruppert, Michael C., *Crossing the Rubicon: The Decline of the American Empire at the End of the Age of Oil*. New Society Publishers, 2004.

Russel, Dick & Jesse Ventura, *63 Documents the Government Doesn't Want you to Read*. Skyhorse Publishing, 2011.

Schechter, Danny, Plunder. *Investigating our Economic Calamity and the Subprime Scandal*. Cosimo Books, 2008.

Schulte, Thorsten, *Silber das bessere Gold*. Kopp Verlag, 2010.

Shiller, Robert J., *Irrational Exuberance*. Princeton University Press, 2000.

Shilling, Gary A., *Deflation: How to Survive and Thrive in the Coming Wave of Deflation*. McGraw-Hill, 1999.

Simmons, Matthew R., *Twilight in the Desert: The Coming Saudi Oil Shock and the World Economy*. John Wiley & Sons, 2005.

Stiglitz, Joseph E., *Globalization and Its Discontents*. W. W. Norton & Company, 2003.

Surowiecki, James, *The Wisdom of Crowds: Why the Many are Smarter than the Few*. Little Brown, 2004.

Sutton, Antony C., *America's Secret Establishment: An Introduction to the Order of Skull & Bones*. Trine Day, 2002.

Sutton, Antony C., *The War on Gold*. '76 Press, 1977.

Sutton, Antony C., *Wall Street and the Bolshevik Revolution*. Buccaneer Books, 1974.

Sutton, Antony C., *Wall Street and the Rise of Hitler*. GSG & Associates, 2002.

Sutton, Antony C. et al., *Flashing Out Skull & Bones*. Millegan, Kris, *Investigations into America's Most Powerful Secret Society*. Trine Day, 2003.

Taleb, Nassim Nicholas, *Fooled by Randomness: The Hidden Role of Chance in Life and in the Markets*. Random House, 2005.

Taylor, James & Warren Shaw, *The Penguin Dictionary of the Third Reich*. Penguin Books, 1997.

Thoren, Theodore R. & Richard F. Warner, *The Truth in Money Book*, Truth In Money, 1984.

Thurow, Lester C., *The Future of Capitalism: How Today's Economic Forces Shape Tomorrow's World*. Penguin Books, 1996.

Treaster, Joseph B., *Paul Volcker: The Making of a Financial Legend*. John Wiley & Sons, 2004.

Warner, Oliver, *English Maritime Writing: Hakluyt to Cook*. Unwin Brothers Limited, 1958.

Weiss, Martin D., *Crash Profits: Make Money When Stocks Sink and Soar!*, John Wiley & Sons, 2003.

Weiss, Martin D., *The Ultimate Depression Survival Guide: Protect your Savings, Boost your Income and Grow Wealthy Even in the Worst of Times*. John Wiley & Sons, 2009.

Weiss, Martin D., *The Ultimate Safe Money Guide: How Everyone 50 and Over Can Protect, Save and Grow Their Money*. John Wiley & Sons, 2002.

Weldon, Gregory T., *Gold Trading Boot Camp: How to Master the Basics and Become a Successful Commodities Investor*. John Wiley & Sons, 2007.

Widdig, Bernd, *Culture and inflation in Weimar Germany*. The University of California Press, 2001.

Yergin, Daniel, *The Prize: The Epic Quest for Oil, Money & Power*. Free Press, 1992.

Zijlstra, Jelle, *Per slot van rekening*. Contact, 1992.

Register